GETTING STARTED WITH DIGITAL COLLECTIONS

ALA Editions purchases fund advocacy, awareness, and accreditation programs for library professionals worldwide.

GETTING STARTED WITH DIGITAL COLLECTIONS

SCALING TO FIT YOUR ORGANIZATION

JANE D. MONSON

 *An imprint of the American Library Association*
CHICAGO / 2017

JANE D. MONSON is currently digital initiatives librarian at the University of Northern Colorado. Previously, she was digital projects librarian at Truman State University in Missouri. She edited the LITA Guide *Jump-Start Your Career as a Digital Librarian* (2013). She is reviews editor for the *Journal of Web Librarianship* and serves on the Resources for College Libraries Editorial Board. Monson holds an MA in library and information science from the University of Iowa.

© 2017 by the American Library Association

Extensive effort has gone into ensuring the reliability of the information in this book; however, the publisher makes no warranty, express or implied, with respect to the material contained herein.

ISBNs
978-0-8389-1543-1 (paper)
978-0-8389-1545-5 (PDF)
978-0-8389-1546-2 (ePub)
978-0-8389-1547-9 (Kindle)

Library of Congress Cataloging-in-Publication Data

Names: Monson, Jane D., 1977- author.
Title: Getting started with digital collections : scaling to fit your organization / Jane D. Monson.
Description: Chicago : ALA Editions, an imprint of the American Library Association, 2017.
Identifiers: LCCN 2016047208 | ISBN 9780838915431 (pbk. : alk. paper) | ISBN 9780838915455 (PDF) | ISBN 9780838915462 (ePub) | ISBN 9780838915479 (Kindle)
Subjects: LCSH: Digital libraries—Management. | Small libraries—Administration. | Library materials—Digitization. | Metadata. | Digital libraries—Collection development. | Copyright and digital preservation. | Digital preservation.
Classification: LCC ZA4080 .M66 2017 | DDC 025.8/4—dc23 LC record available at https://lccn.loc.gov/2016047208

Book design by Kimberly Thornton in the Brandon Grotesque and Utopia typefaces. Cover images: Adobe Stock.

♾ This paper meets the requirements of ANSI/NISO Z39.48-1992 (Permanence of Paper).

Printed in the United States of America

21 20 19 18 17   5 4 3 2 1

CONTENTS

Preface / vii

PART I: MANAGING PROJECTS — 1

1. Digitization at Smaller Institutions 3
2. The Solo Digital Librarian 19
3. Working across Departments 35
4. Working across Institutions 51

PART II: BASIC SKILLS — 65

5. Image Conversion 67
6. Metadata 87
7. Digital Collection Management Systems 111
8. Copyright and Digital Collections 133
9. Preserving Your Digital Assets 151

Glossary / 171

Index / 177

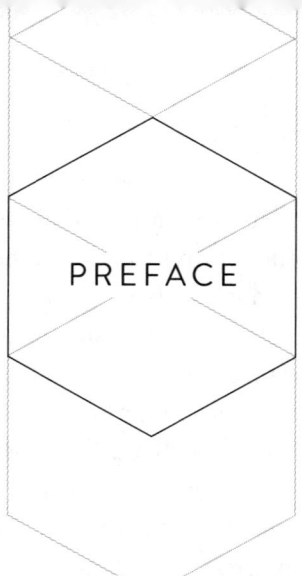

PREFACE

THE IMMENSE CHANGES BROUGHT ABOUT BY THE DIGITAL REVOLUTION ARE still relatively recent in the collective memory, and most of us can recall a time when libraries, archives, and museums were strictly places to be visited, physical destinations first and foremost. Now that the Digital Age is well underway this reality has shifted, as these institutions are able to harness the Internet to bring their collections directly to users, wherever they may be. Once novel, this level of service has become the expectation of a public that is accustomed to having all manner of information at its fingertips at all times.

Even for the largest cultural heritage institutions, this expectation can be difficult to meet—many have been digitizing materials for years and have yet to make much of a dent in their overall holdings. But smaller institutions face a unique challenge. They may have been unable to jump on the digitization bandwagon at its beginning due to competing priorities or lack of resources, and are now struggling to get a digitization program in place to meet the evolving needs and expectations of their own users. The larger digitization conversation, which has centered mainly around the larger institutions, has now progressed to the point that a novice will have trouble wading through news of the latest innovations and acronyms to piece together the basic knowledge they need to get started.

As a graduate student in library and information science, I was lucky enough to receive a comprehensive education in digitization fundamentals through a specialized curriculum that included hands-on project work in a well-established digitization program at a large academic library. This experience gave me the ability to step into a position as a solo digital librarian at a small academic institution that was starting a brand-new digitization program from scratch. But administrators at many smaller institutions cannot, and perhaps do not want to, hire a designated digitization professional to oversee the creation of their first digital collections. And frankly, they don't need to. Nonexperts can accomplish the task just as successfully when equipped with some fundamental knowledge and the right tools.

As with many endeavors, the hard part is often figuring out where to start. This book provides an entry point for librarians, archivists, and curators who are new to digitization. It aims to assemble in one place the key information necessary to get a digitization program off the ground. It focuses on the needs of professionals at small and midsize cultural heritage institutions who do not have previous experience with digital collections and who may be working with limitations related to money, staffing, and technology. The book is divided into two parts: "Managing Projects," which provides strategies for completing digitization projects at smaller institutions, succeeding as a solo digital collections manager, and working collaboratively both within and outside your institution; and "Basic Skills," which defines important terminology and outlines best practices for digital image conversion, metadata creation, hardware and software selection, copyright compliance, and digital preservation.

This book is also meant to be a jumping-off point for further learning, since no single volume can provide you with all the information you may need or want to know. After reading it, my hope is that you will have a strong grounding in digitization fundamentals, as well as a solid grasp of the resources available to assist you as you move forward.

Jane D. Monson

PART I

MANAGING PROJECTS

DIGITIZATION AT SMALLER INSTITUTIONS

Digitization HAS BEEN ONE OF THE MOST FREQUENTLY USED buzzwords in the cultural heritage sector since the early twenty-first century, when the activity really began to take off in libraries, archives, and museums. While well-funded, cutting-edge institutions started their nascent digitization programs in the 1990s, it wasn't until the mid-2000s that a tipping point was reached—this is according to a 2005 Association of College and Research Libraries survey of academic libraries, which found a nearly tenfold increase in the number of digital collections reported since the previous year (Raab 2007). These days everyone's doing it, or so it seems, and for many institutions—the large public and research libraries, museums, and archives of the world—it almost seems as good as done. If you look at the websites of institutions like the Library of Congress, the British Museum, or a Big Ten university library, you may find thousands if not millions of digitized objects in nicely designed collections, complete with detailed descriptive records and likely a slew of "added value" features such as OCR (optical character recognition) for full-text searching; images that can be zoomed, panned, and cropped; social media integration; or interactive multimedia such as maps and time lines. These collections represent many years and man-hours of work, usually involving specialists who are dedicated to their creation, and often entire departments of such specialists.

Often in the parlance of digital librarians and other technologists there is talk of "scaling," referring to whether or not a process scales up to a larger level of magnitude. But in the case of digitization at smaller institutions, such as public and college libraries and local archives, museums, and historical societies, the better question may be whether the approach of larger institutions scales down. These are the places where digitization efforts may still be getting off the ground, and where librarians, archivists, and curators are seeking out the best ways to get started with digitizing their collections. They may be feeling pressure to "catch up" to larger organizations—indeed, according to a 2010 report by the Online Computer Library Center, one of the most challenging issues in special collections and archives was the "implicit mandate to put as much material as possible online, and as soon as possible" (Dooley and Luce 2010). If anything, this expectation has only grown stronger with time.

But can small and medium-sized institutions successfully follow the model of larger ones when it comes to digitization processes and workflows? In some ways the answer is yes, but in many ways it is no. While the basics may remain the same—scanning images, creating metadata, loading objects into a digital collections management system (DCMS)—the details of these activities, and the groundwork that must be laid in order to allow these activities to happen, may vary quite a bit between institutions of different sizes. This chapter looks at the ways in which digitization at smaller institutions is unique, and examines special considerations that may need to be taken into account by librarians, archivists, and curators when embarking on smaller-scale digitization projects. It also explores the advantages that smaller institutions may have when it comes to digitizing their collections.

Why Digitize?

But first things first—before we look too closely at the hows of smaller-scale digitization, let's briefly discuss the whys. And what, exactly, do we mean when we say "digitization"? For our purposes, we will define digitization as the reformatting of physical or analog materials to create digital surrogates or facsimiles. This is done using technologies such as scanners and digital cameras. There are many types of materials that libraries, museums, and archives might choose to digitize, among them photographs and other types of images, manuscripts, maps, printed music, recorded music and oral histories, videos, slides, microfilm, and three-dimensional objects.

There are various reasons an institution may decide to digitize its holdings. In the early years of digital collection building, the emphasis was almost exclusively on access: to put digital materials online so they can be found and used, in order to make the materials more broadly, quickly, and efficiently accessible (Levy 2000). Increased accessibility continues to be a very important objective, particularly for collections that may be "hidden" or obscured from the public in their physical form, for example uncataloged or noncirculating archival materials. Allowing ubiquitous access to collections via the Web allows them to be discovered and utilized by a much broader audience than only those users who are willing and able to visit an institution to view its unique local holdings in person.

Digitization should, first and foremost, meet an institution's obligation to make its collections accessible. However, Stephen Chapman makes the important distinction that making collections Internet-accessible is not the same as making them user-accessible. "Before emulating the policies and practices of a peer institution, ask whether its programs have been configured to serve comparable audiences and audience needs" (Chapman 2004). It may not be appropriate for a rural public library, for example, to model its selection and digitization strategies after that of a large research university, since its patron base will likely be quite different. Accessibility encompasses not just making material available in digital form, but understanding the organization's users and the uses they will make of the available information.

A second reason to digitize is for preservation purposes. Creating digital surrogates can serve to indirectly protect fragile or brittle physical materials by providing an alternative means of access, thereby minimizing handling and further damage to the original (that is, if demand for the original item does not increase due to heightened awareness caused by the availability of the digital surrogate, a possible side effect). Digitization for preservation, as this approach is known, is not to be confused with digital preservation, which can essentially be defined as preservation practices that are applied to digital materials that are either born digital or reformatted from analog media. Digital preservation is an important step in the process of digitization, and one that will be discussed at length in chapter 9. It is important to note that digital surrogates should not be considered replacements for analog originals, which have intrinsic value and compared with which even the best-quality digital image represents a loss of information (Besser 2003).

Finally, there is the previously mentioned "added value" factor. Digitization can provide a means of enriching materials and collections with features that assist users in utilizing and understanding them in new and novel ways. This may be as straightforward as functionality that allows users to select digital objects across collections and save them into their own, personalized digital collections, or as sophisticated as text encoding that permits scholars to mine texts for new insights regarding their content and meaning. Data visualization is another way that digital materials can be brought to life, allowing users to better understand the context of a digital collection by placing the data in a visual context (think interactive graphs, charts, time lines, and maps). Digitization can create new ways for information to be displayed, analyzed, and understood that may be difficult or impossible in the original analog form.

Aside from these three basic goals, there are secondary objectives to be gained from digitization. As Terence K. Huwe points out, digital collections have the potential to create excitement among patrons, and the process of digitizing these collections can be a good way for institutions to attract funding, political support, and patron attention (Huwe 2013). Particularly for smaller organizations that serve the public sector, digitization of unique local holdings can be a smart public relations move and can further institutional goals to satisfy patron needs. This is to say nothing of patron expectations, of course. We live in an era when patrons may anticipate, and indeed demand, that information be made available to them in virtual form. This provides incentive for digitization projects, but it can also leave cultural heritage institutions stuck "somewhere in the middle . . . facing an audience which expects to step through a perfectly designed gateway into a virtual world where everything is available online" (Walsh 2013). This expectation can create particular challenges for small institutions that may already have significant hurdles to surmount when it comes to creating sustainable digitization programs.

Patrons are often surprised to learn that universal digitization has not been achieved for all or most library, archive, and museum content. After many years of hard work, even small institutions may have only a small percentage of their holdings converted to digital. It is important to remember that digitization is usually a slow and steady process that involves a good deal of design and planning prior to execution. Projects often take longer than originally anticipated, and a good rule of thumb when planning for new digitization initiatives is to allow for a time frame twice as long as initially projected. This is particularly true for first-time projects; as experience is gained, so also is speed. It is also generally the case that smaller institutions may see slower progress, at least at first, for reasons outlined later in the chapter.

When asking "Why digitize?" it is important to keep in mind the specific mission of the institution. As David M. Levy emphasizes, more information is not always better and digital libraries cannot be all things to all people (Levy 2000). In the same vein as Chapman's emphasis on user accessibility, an academic library serving students and researchers may have very different motives and aims than a public library or museum when it comes to selecting materials for digitization, and overarching institutional goals should be adhered to when planning which items to digitize. Factors to consider include which items are perceived to have the most demand from the patron population and which items best reflect the unique holdings of the specific institution.

Digitization at Smaller Institutions: How It's Unique

In his article "College Librarians and the University-Library Syndrome," Evan Ira Farber observed a "pattern of attitudes which cause college librarians . . . to think of their libraries in terms of university libraries and imitate practices, attitudes and objectives" of these larger organizations (Farber 1974). This tendency Farber dubbed "university-library syndrome," and he stressed that differences between these two types of institutions should be kept in mind if college libraries are to achieve their goals. Access to electronic information has narrowed the gulf between college and university libraries considerably since Farber wrote his article, but the "syndrome" he describes may be alive and well in another form in the era of digitization. It is tempting for librarians, archivists, and curators to look to larger institutions as models when embarking on their first forays into digital collection building. However, there are differences that must be kept in mind if smaller institutions are to achieve their digitization goals.

At the same time, there is the growing expectation that smaller institutions will provide the same level of service as larger ones, and this provides a unique challenge. In the area of academia, "small academic libraries are challenged to continue essential legacy services while ratcheting up new projects that will enable students and faculty to engage in twenty-first-century research and learning . . . Although resources for small college libraries pale in comparison to those at research university libraries, many of the same services are expected by faculty and students" (Doherty and Piper 2015). This is arguably the case for all types of cultural heritage institutions, where global online access to content has become the expectation of the public at large.

One commonality of smaller institutions is that they often have fewer resources when it comes to money, staff, and infrastructure. Successful digitization projects rely on all three of these elements, and a lack in any area can serve as a major hindrance to overall progress. Thus, smaller institutions often have to get creative when it comes to marshaling the resources necessary to digitize their collections. It is also the case that every individual digitization project is unique, and that resources will need to be allocated on a project-by-project basis. The three areas of money, staff, and infrastructure are discussed in more detail in the following sections.

MONEY

Money, or lack thereof, is a deciding factor in numerous aspects of digitization. Many small and midsized institutions must deal with less-than-adequate funding in multiple areas of operation, and this often carries over to digitization initiatives. Funding is perhaps the greatest challenge when it comes to these projects, as it affects every other aspect, including staffing and infrastructure. Money is needed to hire project staff, purchase scanning equipment, license necessary software, and arrange for short- and long-term digital file storage. Researching costs and determining that an adequate revenue stream is available prior to beginning a digitization project are essential first steps.

The good news is that digitization projects can be completed on a shoestring budget. In the lowest-cost scenario, an organization's preexisting scanning technology can be repurposed for digital projects or a new flatbed scanner purchased for a reasonable cost; existing staff can be reassigned to digitization tasks; and free, open source software can be utilized to deliver digital objects and metadata to users. While this bare-bones approach is not always ideal, it is possible to create digital collections with a minimal outlay of monetary resources.

The bad news is that less money spent may lead to lower quality in the final product, and the bare-bones approach can sometimes create more problems than it solves. This will be illustrated in more depth in later chapters discussing DCMSs and digital preservation. But suffice it to say that many institutions choose to spend more than may seem strictly necessary because paying more, for example, for a commercial DCMS rather than a free option, can save time, headaches, and (yes) more money down the road. This is not an endorsement of one option over another, merely an acknowledgment that dealing with funding issues will inevitably lead to trade-offs that an institution will need to weigh carefully in the planning stages, and that will vary considerably due to individual institutional needs. A dispassionate and level-headed examination of necessary requirements versus desired features and functionalities, coupled with careful research into the available options, will set the stage for a project that makes successful use of available monetary resources.

One avenue that many smaller institutions pursue in order to address monetary shortfalls is to apply for grant funding. There are many funding opportunities available at the national, state, and local levels that can be used to seed a digitization project or program. The National Endowment for the Humanities, the Institute of Museum and Library Services, and the National Historical Publications and Records Commission are federal organizations that offer grant funding specifically for digitization initiatives. Private foundations that have an interest in the specific subject domain related to the materials you want to digitize may also be sources of funding (for example, you may be able to make a case to a national anthropological association for funding the digitization of a noted archaeologist's field notes). When looking for grant funding, it is usually advisable to focus on discrete, one-time purchases such as scanning equipment or servers. This is because many costs related to digital collections are ongoing, for example software licenses and staff salaries, and once a grant ends it may be a challenge to replace funds for these continuing costs with those from a homegrown source. Keep in mind, though, that hardware and equipment will also need to be replaced at some point in the future.

Unfortunately, grant funding for digitization may be more difficult to secure in the current climate than it once was. Marshall Breeding argues that digitizing collections is no longer an especially "noteworthy" activity, and that libraries seeking external funding for digitizing will have to work harder than ever to present a convincing argument (Breeding 2014). For this reason, it is a wise goal to make digitization activities part of the regular organizational budget, rather than relying too heavily on outside sources of funding. However, grant monies can be invaluable for getting your digitization program off the ground.

A cost-saving path that a large number of smaller institutions follow is to join a local, regional, state, or national consortium. The ability to share costs across multiple institutions is a highly appealing prospect, and for some small institutions this cost-sharing may be the deciding factor that enables them to pursue any digitization program at all. There are many reasons why the consortium route is advantageous for small and medium-sized institutions, and these are looked at more closely in chapter 4, which examines cross-institutional collaboration.

STAFFING

Following funding, staffing is perhaps the second greatest digitization challenge for smaller organizations. In ideal circumstances, a cadre of full-time staff members would be assigned solely to digital projects, possibly forming a unit or department dedicated to digitization initiatives. There would be people whose positions would be devoted to tasks such as project management, metadata creation, collection development, software and hardware management, web design, and production work (creating digital objects and uploading them to a DCMS). These and other tasks combine to make digitization a complex and multifaceted process, requiring that disparate areas of expertise come together in order to ensure success.

This does not mean that if your institution lacks such a team of people, you are out of luck when it comes to starting a digitization program. The above is the best-case scenario, and one that may be necessary at large institutions in order to deal with the high volume of content being digitized (not to mention various levels of bureaucracy that may exist). However, the model of a dedicated digitization unit is often neither feasible nor practical for smaller institutions, for reasons linked to money and infrastructure. Small, stand-alone digitization projects may even suffer from this type of model, being bogged down by too many hands. Many small and medium-sized institutions have successfully started and maintained a digitization program with one or fewer dedicated full-time staff members, but as with most other aspects of small-scale digitization, the task requires flexibility and creativity.

For the smaller institution, the best-case scenario for starting a digitization program involves hiring or repurposing a position for a digital librarian, someone who is tasked solely with planning and managing digital projects. Ideally, this person would strategize how to get the overall project off the ground, formulate effective workflows and procedures, and maintain these processes over time. He or she may conduct hands-on activities such as metadata creation or quality control, or merely serve as a project manager and facilitator for those who do. The digital librarian may not even be a full-time staff member, but he or she should be tasked solely with administering and overseeing digital projects (one staffing model that does not work as well is to add project management to the tasks of someone who is already working full-time in another area). It is important to have at least one person who is responsible for taking the lead in this manner, in order to ensure smooth and efficient project work. A more in-depth look at the work of the digital librarian, with a focus on those who work more-or-less "solo," is the topic of chapter 2.

It may be tempting to believe that hiring a digital librarian will take care of all of the staffing needs of the smaller institution; however, this is not necessarily the case if one desires to see projects completed in a timely and efficient manner. At organizations of all sizes, digitization is a team effort and collaboration is key. Yet the large institution staffing model outlined above is often not realistic for the small or medium-sized institution. Where, then, does the manpower come from? In most cases, it is necessary to repurpose staff from other areas and reassign to them digitization duties (perhaps even reassigning someone to the role of digital librarian, who may then have to learn the job from scratch). This requires making digitization a priority at the institutional level, because coordination between units, departments, and people is vital. Information pertaining to existing staff roles and suggestions for how to best repurpose them for digitization activities can be found in chapter 3.

Reassigning staff duties reflects an overall need for a collaborative approach to digitization. This is true of programs at large institutions, where the aforementioned cadre of specialists would work together to shepherd a project through to completion. Again, this model may not be feasible for the library or archive with one or fewer digital experts. In these cases, it is usually required that the digital librarian or designated project manager gather together a group of colleagues who have intersecting or adjacent areas of expertise in order to both advise on and execute projects. Collaboration at the interdepartmental and consortium levels is explored further in chapters 3 and 4.

INFRASTRUCTURE

Rounding out the triad of issues faced by small and medium-sized libraries is that of technical infrastructure, including things such as scanning equipment, software, and servers. Obviously, these items can be expensive to purchase and maintain, which is where the challenge lies for smaller institutions with limited budgets. As is the case with funding and staffing, a little creativity and flexibility can go a long way toward solving the problems that may be confronted in this area. And luckily, the costs of storage and equipment have dropped dramatically over the past decade or so.

At the most basic level, any institution launching a digitization program will need to invest in one or more scanners—at least, any organization wishing to digitize still images, which are often the easiest starting point and are therefore the focus of the digital conversion chapter in this book (chapter 5). It may be possible to avoid such a purchase on stand-alone digitization projects, where it may be an option to outsource or share equipment with another institution. However, if an institution intends to create multiple digital collections over a prolonged period of time, it is worth the investment to purchase equipment for in-house scanning.

Depending on the level of output anticipated and the number of staff members available to work on scanning, multiple machines will likely be needed. For a very small operation, one scanner may be enough, at least for the short term. It may be a good idea to start small, for example by purchasing one image scanner that is dedicated to digital projects, and experimenting with it to determine the rate of speed at which you or your staff are able to produce digital files. Don't be surprised if it is a slower process than you had expected, and you determine that additional scanners are required to maximize efficiency.

Grant funding may be a good option for minimizing the expense of scanning equipment, since as mentioned before, granting agencies will more readily provide funding for one-time purchases such as hardware than for ongoing costs such as software or staffing. For example, Library Services and Technology Act funds administered through your state library can often be used for digitization equipment purchases. If you belong to a consortium or are participating in some other type of collaborative project, it may also be possible to share equipment with a neighboring institution. This solution, however, is only advisable for discrete, one-off projects and not for long-term, sustained digitization programs. In the case of the latter, the efficiency provided by dedicated on-site machines is usually worth the trade-off in cost.

Other important aspects of infrastructure that are crucial for digital collection building include the underlying web servers and networks used to store and deliver digital content. A detailed examination of technical architecture for digital collections is beyond the scope of this book, and for our purposes it is necessary only to understand the basics. When planning your digital collections program, it is important to involve information technology (IT) professionals at your organization who have a good understanding of server and local network management and the capabilities of your institution's technical infrastructure.

Large institutions usually have the benefit of dedicated IT departments where local servers and software may be housed and managed by full-time technologists, thus providing an on-site location for file storage and delivery of content on the Web. If you have the resources to support it, you may decide to store and deliver your digital collections in-house from a local server. The basic infrastructure requirements of this model are extensible server hardware that can expand with the need for greater processing, memory, and hard disk storage; software that supports open standards; and a fast network connection (Tennant 1998). This may be the best solution for institutions that have access to a robust existing technology infrastructure and dedicated technical staff to manage it.

In recent years, another model has emerged which offers a good alternative to the local computing model outlined above: cloud computing. Cloud computing provides access to software applications, digital storage, and other technical resources through services that can be accessed via the Web, meaning that users do not need to purchase and maintain their own network resources. The official National Institute of Standards and Technology definition states:

> Cloud computing is a model for enabling ubiquitous, convenient, on-demand network access to a shared pool of configurable computing

resources (e.g., networks, servers, storage, applications and services) that can be rapidly provisioned and released with minimal management effort or service provider interaction. (NIST 2011)

Cloud computing can ease the burden on smaller institutions that may lack the resources to effectively operate servers and network components that require a high level of technical expertise, allowing them to step away from the intricacies of hardware and software management that larger institutions may be better equipped to handle. Cloud computing can also be a more cost-effective option, as cloud providers benefit from economies of scale that they can then pass on to their customers. Running digital infrastructure on the cloud may make sense for institutions that are starting their digitization programs from scratch and do not have the monetary and staffing resources to invest in an in-house data center. Denis Galvin and Mang Sun recommend that projects using software like Omeka (a free, open source web publishing platform that is often used to collect, preserve, and present small-scale digital collections) are good candidates for the cloud (Galvin and Sun 2012)

Galvin and Sun also point out that all of the same rules that apply to physical hardware apply to a cloud server (ibid. 2012). This reminds us that, as with all technology, there are drawbacks to cloud-based services. For example, if there is a major problem in a cloud data center, then you may be one client among thousands and may not be first in line. Having specialists in-house to deal with major problems costs money up front, but it may end up saving more in the long-term (Carson, Botter, and Krujelskis 2013). Furthermore, running your own programs and applications on the cloud does not negate the need for local technical expertise. It may be feasible to have your own instance of a free, open source DCMS running on a cloud server, but IT personnel or library technologists will still be required to install and manage the software and keep the repository up and running.

In the event that you lack the technical infrastructure to host digital collections either locally or in the cloud, a third option is to contract with a vendor that will provide data storage and a DCMS, all hosted remotely on its servers, along with technical support. Commercial DCMS such as CONTENTdm and bepress operate this way, and there are also third-party service providers that will operate open source repository software such as Omeka or Islandora using this model (these platforms are explored in more detail in chapter 7). Software hosting is generally a very good option for small institutions, particularly when it is offered to members of a consortium or other group. It allows those creating digital collections to focus their efforts on tasks like content selection, metadata creation, and file reformatting instead of setting up, managing, and maintaining hardware and software. There are, of course, drawbacks to using hosted repository solutions as well, and these are discussed in chapter 7.

Advantages of Smaller Institutions

As the previous sections illustrate, there are multiple ways that smaller institutions may be at a disadvantage when it comes to getting digital projects done. The greatest concern for small libraries usually lies in having very limited resources. However, there are some ways that smaller size can be beneficial. When getting started with digitization projects, it's important not to let your organization's perceived deficits overshadow its strengths.

Smaller organizations may have an advantage when it comes to digital collection building because they often have large amounts of unique local content, for example local history collections at public libraries or historical societies. This is the type of material that lends itself particularly well to digitization because it may be highly used in its physical form and will benefit from both increased accessibility and digitization as a preservation measure. Smaller institutions may also have greater local connections that can be tapped into for completing digitization projects. These may include the general public, volunteers, and Friends groups. The knowledge of those who are familiar with local history, people, and events can be invaluable when performing tasks such as metadata creation. Crowdsourcing, the process of getting work or funding from a crowd of people who are online, is one way that local communities have contributed to digitization projects. These projects have generally involved enlisting "the crowd" for assistance in identifying and describing the contents of digitized images and other resources. (However, it's important to remember that volunteers aren't catalogers; trained staff should be utilized as intermediaries to ensure that metadata is accurate and conforms to accepted standards.)

Farber identifies several ways that smaller institutions may have a leg up in general over larger ones in terms of efficiency and innovation. They may have relative clarity of institutional goals, a more manageable size, less bureaucracy, and more independence (Farber 2000). Doherty and Piper echo these sentiments and contend that, at least when it comes to academic libraries, smaller institutions can be "more agile and quick to adopt new technologies and workflows with compact communication networks, legacy flexibility in job functions, and fewer layers of bureaucracy and cultural differences with which to contend" (Doherty and Piper 2015). All of these advantages can carry over into the realm of digitization and allow for increased productivity and creativity.

Karen Calhoun identifies four key challenges facing digital libraries, one of which is community engagement, asserting that deep engagement with the communities that digital libraries have been meant to serve is uneven (Calhoun 2014). Why do some digital libraries have a distinctive impact on their communities, while others are more or less ignored? Similarly, Hamilton defines a sustainable digital library as one that is considered essential by the community it serves (Hamilton 2004). An advantage of the smaller library, archive, or museum is that it may be better placed to meet the challenges of community engagement and social sustainability through deep and long-standing connections with the local population. A smaller institution can provide access to content that is highly valued by the community it serves by capitalizing on its unique local holdings. It is these previously hidden or inaccessible collections that often attract the most users, who may feel that they have a personal stake in the preservation and curation of these particular cultural assets, assets that have few or no substitutes elsewhere.

Finally, R. David Lankes asserts that "the mission of librarians is to improve society through facilitating knowledge creation in their communities" (Lankes 2011). This concept of "participatory librarianship" is well served by the smaller library or other knowledge institution that makes its digitized holdings available to the public. Through crowdsourcing or merely by enabling access to these materials, institutions can leverage their strong local connections and give users the ability to reuse and repurpose content that is especially meaningful to them. The types of collections held by smaller institutions, particularly those related to local history, tend to lend themselves well to this type of endeavor.

Final Thoughts

Digitization as a whole is an activity that involves many moving parts, and these will be discussed at length in later chapters. This complexity can pose many challenges, and for smaller institutions these challenges may be amplified by limited knowledge and resources. If you are at a small or medium-sized institution and are just getting started with your digitization program, you'll want to carefully examine your available resources and strategize how best to organize them in order to maximize their potential. You may not have very much wiggle room when it comes to money, staff, and infrastructure, and you will most likely be required to muster a good deal of creativity, flexibility, and resourcefulness.

But just because digitization can present special issues for small institutions, this doesn't mean that it isn't worth pursuing. The benefits to the institution and its patrons will generally far outweigh any difficulties that may arise during planning and execution, and once the initial hurdles are overcome, your digitization program can proceed as smoothly and efficiently as any other core service. As with any new endeavor, initial investments in research and planning will pay dividends down the road. At the same time, don't be afraid to make mistakes, since very little in the world of digitization is irreversible. Strive to meet the standards, best practices, and guidelines that are outlined in this book, but recognize too that perfection is not the ultimate goal. Digitization at smaller institutions requires finding a balance that works for you and your users.

REFERENCES

Besser, Howard. 2003. *Introduction to Imaging, Revised Edition.* Los Angeles: Getty Research Institute. www.getty.edu/research/publications/electronic_publications/introimages/.

Breeding, Marshall. 2014. "Shifting to the Cloud: Reshaping Library Technology Infrastructure." *Computers in Libraries* 34, no. 2 (March): 26.

Calhoun, Karen. 2014. *Exploring Digital Libraries: Foundations, Practice, Prospects.* London: Facet.

Carson, Pamela, Kathleen Botter, and Stephen Krujelskis. 2013. "Going to the Cloud vs. Doing It In-House." *Computers in Libraries* 32, no. 6 (July/August): 4–10.

Chapman, Stephen. 2004. "Techniques for Creating Sustainable Digital Collections." *Library Technology Reports* 40, no. 5 (September/October).

Doherty, Brian, and Alison Piper. 2015. "Creating a New Organizational Structure for a Small Academic Library: The Merging of Technical Services and Access Services." *Technical Services Quarterly* 32, no. 2 (March): 160–72. doi: 10.1080/07317131.2015.998466.

Dooley, Jackie M., and Katherine Luce. 2010. *Taking Our Pulse: The OCLC Research Survey of Special Collections and Archives.* Dublin, OH: OCLC Research. www.oclc.org/content/dam/research/publications/library/2010/2010-11.pdf.

Farber, Evan Ira. 1974. "College Librarians and the University-Library Syndrome." In *The Academic Library: Essays in Honor of Guy R. Lyle,* edited by Evan Ira Farber and Ruth Walling, 12–23. Metuchen, NJ: Scarecrow.

Galvin, Denis, and Mang Sun. 2012. "Avoiding the Death Zone: Choosing and Running a Library Project in the Cloud." *Library Hi Tech* 40, no. 3 (August): 418–27.

Hamilton, Val. 2004. "Sustainability for Digital Libraries." *Library Review* 53, no. 8: 392–95. doi: 10.1108/00242530410556210.

Huwe, Terence K. 2013. "The Social Life of Digital Collections." *Computers in Libraries* 33, no. 9 (November): 23–25.

Lankes, R. David. 2011. *The Atlas of New Librarianship.* Cambridge, MA: MIT Press.

Levy, David M. 2000. "Digital Libraries and the Problem of Purpose." *D-Lib Magazine* 6, no. 1 (January). doi: 10.1045/january2000-levy.

National Institute of Standards and Technology (NIST). 2011. "Final Version of NIST Cloud Computing Definition Published." www.nist.gov/itl/csd/cloud-102511.cfm.

Raab, Christopher. 2007. "From the ACRL 13th National Conference: Collaborative Solutions to Digitization for College Library Special Collections." *College and Undergraduate Libraries* 14, no. 4: 37–48.

Tennant, Roy. 1998. "Digital Library Infrastructure." *Library Journal* 123, no. 11 (June): 32, 34.

Walsh, David. 2013. "Digitization: Surely It Can't Be That Difficult?" *Insights* 26, no. 3 (November): 277–81.

THE SOLO DIGITAL LIBRARIAN

WHILE DIGITIZATION PROJECTS HAVE BECOME INCREASingly common in libraries, archives, and museums over the past twenty years, there is still a sense of mystery surrounding the role of professionals who specialize in these activities. The public and even colleagues in the cultural heritage sector often do not have a clear understanding of what exactly these people do, or why their work is important. The functions of professionals with more common job titles such as cataloger, reference librarian, archivist, or curator are generally more familiar, having been steeped in decades or even centuries of tradition. But throw out the term *digital librarian* or any variety of associated monikers such as *digital archivist, repository manager*, or *metadata specialist*, and you may well be greeted with a blank look. At best, these professionals may be understood as the ones who "scan things." Of course, we know that there is much more to it than that.

This is one reason why working on digitization projects can sometimes be a rather isolating experience. Not only is there no long-standing frame of reference in the public imagination for such a role, but digitization professionals are often hidden from view by the behind-the-scenes nature of their work. (For the purposes of this chapter we will refer to these professionals as *digital librarians,* regardless of whether they work in a library, archive, museum, or other type of cultural heritage institution.) Digital librarians may also be more likely than other information professionals to work in literal isolation, especially if they are at a small institution or one with an undeveloped digitization program. They may be the "first of their kind," brought in to jump-start a nascent digitization program where none existed before. Or they may be doing double-duty by conducting digitization activities in addition to their regular work as specialists in some other area. Smaller institutions are less likely to have a unit or department dedicated to digital services that is well-integrated into the structure of the overall organization, and administrators may have difficulty determining exactly where a digital librarian fits into the organization chart. A niche may be carved out to fit the digital librarian into an existing department, or he or she may exist as a free-floating entity, a lone wolf within the institution.

This chapter examines the experience of the solo digital librarian, who may be the only person doing this type of work at his or her institution. This person is reformatting expert, metadata creator, copyright specialist, digital preservationist, webmaster, and project manager all rolled into one. He or she may be in charge of evaluating scanning equipment, selecting and implementing a DCMS, and training and supervising others in the use of both. While digitization professionals at large institutions often specialize in a particular area of expertise such as metadata, the solo digital librarian is expected to be a jack-of-all-trades, incorporating a wide variety of knowledge and skills into his or her work, and looked to by others in the organization to be the expert in all of them. As one might expect, this can be a challenging position to be in. The solo digital librarian must learn to juggle the demands of a wide range of tasks and duties.

Though sometimes difficult, solo digital librarianship can also be highly rewarding due to the varied nature of the job and the independence and autonomy it can provide. It offers opportunities to learn a wide range of different skills. McGlone describes the day-to-day life of the digital librarian as varied and exciting, filled with learning opportunities and chances to refine expertise in areas such as technology, project management, and collaboration and outreach (McGlone 2013). One must take a disciplined approach, however, in order to reap the rewards of such an opportunity. Making a concerted effort to develop the skills outlined in this chapter will help you be successful in solo digitization work.

Important Skills

If you are the only person at your institution assigned to work on digital projects, and especially if you are just starting out in this area, you will probably feel at least somewhat overwhelmed initially. You might wonder how you will manage to do all of the different tasks involved in creating and launching a digital collection. In addition to the concrete knowledge that you will need—concepts and skills that are covered in the second half of this book, such as reformatting analog materials to digital and creating a metadata schema—there are also a number of soft skills that, when cultivated, can go a long way toward helping you achieve your goals.

ABILITY TO DELEGATE

Before you get very far into your work, there is one crucial step to take: get help! Even at the smallest of institutions, the solo digital librarian cannot do it alone—at least, not if progress is to be made at more than a snail's pace. Rather than trying to do everything yourself, it is far more efficient to enlist the help of others, whether they are staff, student workers, or volunteers. In order to effectively manage digital projects, you will need to delegate certain time-consuming and easily learned tasks such as scanning materials, creating simple metadata, and uploading digital files to a DCMS. With a minimum amount of training, these types of routine jobs can generally be done by anyone who possesses very basic computer skills. This will free you up to perform higher-level tasks, such as material selection, metadata schema design, and quality control. Of course, you will need to be proficient in the routine tasks in order to manage others who perform them, so for your initial projects it's a good idea to go through the steps of executing them yourself. Once you have them mastered, you can assign them to others and concentrate more on building the other skills that follow.

You may decide to train individual support workers in all digitization tasks so they can step into a project at any stage, or you may have workers specialize in specific jobs like scanning or metadata creation. There are advantages to both approaches. Workers who focus solely on one type of assignment across all projects can become especially skilled at that task, completing it more efficiently and precisely. At the same time, there's much to be said for providing a sense of variety for digitization support staff. Rote tasks like scanning can quickly become monotonous, and while some workers may not mind the tedium, others may lose interest and motivation if not allowed a diversity of experience. Giving support workers a role in all stages of a project can also encourage a greater sense of ownership and investment in the final product.

INTEREST IN TECHNOLOGY

The digital librarian can be described as "an amalgam of the librarian and the web professional," who tends to have a very broad set of technical and professional skills (McGlone 2013). Whether you have a previous background in libraries, archives, or museums, you will find that this basic definition applies—you will be combining your traditional set of professional skills with an array of newer, technology-based ones. But doing digitization projects doesn't require one to have a background in computer science or programming. Having limited experience with these subjects does not preclude one from engaging in digitization activities at all. While a basic working knowledge of computers and the Internet is needed, it's more important to have a certain amount of openness to and interest in technology, especially as it pertains to online resources and the Web. An attitude of resistance or even indifference to new technology and trends such as social media will not serve those who wish to successfully engage in digitization.

This is not to say that you need to become a "techie" or even a technology enthusiast, but you will do well to make an effort to learn about and keep abreast of evolving issues and developments in the world of online computing. You need not become a web coder or designer, but understanding the basic concepts surrounding the structure and use of markup languages like Hyper-Text Markup Language (HTML), Cascading Style Sheets (CSS), and Extensible Markup Language (XML) will at the very least help you to converse with others who use these tools. You will also have a better grasp of what underlies the DCMS or other software you may use to deliver your collections on the Web. You may end up learning more than you ever thought you'd care to know about such topics as server configuration and open source software, but you will also find that the more you learn, the more interesting and accessible these subjects become. As you develop your skills and knowledge, you will also be able to increase the level of control you have over your digital collections and the way they are delivered to users.

In a post on the Library of Congress blog *The Signal,* Bill LeFurgy addresses the question of which skills are essential for a digital archivist or librarian.

He writes that while knowledge of programming, formats, and standards is important, "deep technical expertise is optional . . . the most important thing is a basic understanding of how the different system parts—both automated and manual—contribute to doing the job at hand" (LeFurgy 2011). Having a holistic understanding of all of the moving parts involved in digitization, and how they work together, is just as important as being an expert in any particular technology. Aim to develop a well-rounded awareness of digitization technologies at a broad level, and then explore more in-depth the specific topics that interest you the most. It is not necessary, nor is it feasible, to master all of the technologies you will use.

ABILITY TO LEARN INDEPENDENTLY

It's common these days for academic programs in library science, archival studies, and museum studies to offer coursework, curricula, and practicums designed to prepare students for jobs working with digital collections. But many in the cultural heritage community entered the profession before digitization was a core activity with associated formal training, or they originally specialized in a different area and have found themselves relocated to the world of digital collections, possibly with no colleagues at their institution to guide them. For these people, much of their knowledge has been self-taught. If you are reading this book, you probably have little background or training in digitization or digital collection management. In reading this guide, you are exercising a valuable skill in the digital librarian's toolkit, which is independent learning. Whether you are teaching yourself the basics of digital collection building or you have been trained in the latest technologies, you will need to establish and maintain a habit of autodidacticism, or self-education, to carry on throughout your career. Digital technologies, including hardware, software, file formats, and programming languages, are constantly evolving. The best way to successfully stay abreast of changing practices and systems is to develop a method of self-study that will keep you exposed to advances in the field and allow you to expand your practical skillset.

Luckily, there is an abundance of resources available for those at all levels of experience. Books are often the best place to start for more in-depth coverage of the topics you will be introduced to in later chapters, and numerous guides have been published on all aspects of digitization, from metadata to digital preservation. Books can also be a good starting point if you wish to teach yourself a specific skill, such as web programming with HTML and CSS or database design with Structured Query Language (SQL), but these subjects generally also require a greater degree of hands-on learning to master. Good places to start are websites like Code Academy (www.codeacademy.com), Lynda (www.lynda.com), and W3schools (www.W3schools.com), which offer a variety of online tutorials in web programming and design. For more in-depth training, you may consider enrolling in one of the growing number of MOOCS, or massive open online courses, that are offered by academic institutions around the world, or sign up for a class at your local university or community college.

Professional organizations at the national, state, and regional levels often offer continuing education opportunities through workshops, conferences, and webinars, where you can learn about trends and best practices from your peers in the field. These can be helpful for gaining a sense of how your colleagues at other institutions are implementing their digitization programs, which is particularly valuable if you are the lone digitization professional at your institution. Exposing yourself to projects at similar institutions and understanding how they were or were not successful is one of the most constructive ways to move forward with your own digitization endeavors.

Finally, no program of self-directed learning would be complete without making an effort to follow the professional conversation via formal outlets such as journals and trade publications, and informal ones like blogs and e-mail lists. These sources usually offer the timeliest and most current information about trends and issues in digitization. A list of recommended resources is provided at the end of this chapter.

Depending on how deeply you wish to delve into digitization-related computer skills and technologies, you may need to dedicate a certain amount of your free time to these learning endeavors. For most readers, basic knowledge of the concepts outlined in this book will allow them to engage in simple digital collection building, in the form of creating and managing digital text and image files and making them available via a turnkey software solution. Others may wish to go further by customizing their software, creating scripts to perform automated tasks on metadata and other digital files, or marking up text files using XML to provide enhanced functionalities for users. Learning the necessary web design and programming skills to achieve this level of sophistication with your collections is possible, but it requires time, practice, patience, and commitment.

WILLINGNESS TO EXPERIMENT

Closely aligned with self-directed learning is the ability to try new things and experiment with technologies that you may not be familiar with. There is an element of flexibility that is needed by most professionals to be successful in their jobs, but the solo digital librarian must develop and maintain a particular openness to experimentation in the face of unfamiliar tasks. For example, during the design phase of digital collection building, you will ideally want to evaluate multiple DCMSs. Perhaps you want to try out an open source platform, but are unversed in the process of installing and configuring the necessary software components. Or perhaps the system has been installed, but it is up to you to learn how to use it with no outside training and meager documentation.

In instances such as these, the best course of action is simply to jump into the deep end. One of the most useful skills you can hone is the ability to persist through tasks that may at first seem overwhelming and confusing. One aspect of working in a technology-related field is that there can be a fair degree of uncertainty involved, a lot of trial and error and "trying things out." If you don't have colleagues at your institution to help you, this can be a frustrating part of the job. You will need to develop patience, perseverance, and resourcefulness in order to troubleshoot the questions and issues that will inevitably arise in your day-to-day dealings with technology. You might not succeed at everything you try, but when you do get that software installed or that program running after many hours spent tearing your hair out, the feeling of accomplishment can be very satisfying. The experience and confidence you gain will build on themselves to make it easier to tackle future challenges. Specific advice on troubleshooting technology is included later in the chapter.

ABILITY TO MANAGE MULTIPLE PROJECTS AT VARIOUS STAGES

When you first get started digitizing your collections, you may decide to begin slowly and do one project at a time. This is an entirely appropriate and prudent approach for the beginner; it will allow you to build your skills systematically without becoming overwhelmed. It is helpful when embarking on your first project or two to proceed through the stages of digitization in a more or less linear fashion, beginning with material selection and reformatting and moving on to metadata creation and uploading content to a DCMS. It's also a good idea to do one project at a time until you feel comfortable with the process and confident in your own abilities and those of others who may be assisting you. This way you can avoid making mistakes, such as scanning images at an inappropriate resolution, that will affect content in multiple collections. In other words, it's generally beneficial to polish your skills by proceeding slowly before you kick off your digitization program in earnest.

But once you have gotten your feet wet with a couple of projects in this manner, you will probably want to take a more comprehensive approach to your work. A mature and robust digitization program can be identified by the existence of multiple overlapping projects being conducted simultaneously. After you have put in the time and effort to establish a digitization framework at your institution, you will very likely find no end to the number of collections begging to be undertaken. A long list of potential projects will form, chosen by you or suggested by others, which is a positive development but one that can quickly become daunting. Assuming that you have at this point delegated to others such ongoing tasks as scanning, content upload, and simple metadata creation, you will find your job has shifted to one that is more managerial in nature. Learning how to juggle multiple projects at different stages of completion will become one of your most valuable and necessary skills for keeping a digitization program running efficiently into the future.

To avoid becoming bogged down by the mounting number of projects that may begin to accrue, it's wise to develop a project management strategy. The following are some approaches to consider.

Document: Create documentation to formalize the process of project selection and outline the scope of your digitization program. Draft a digital collection development policy delineating the criteria by which a collection is considered a desirable candidate for digitization. Make these determinations early on and use them to guide future decision-making. For each individual project, document decisions made regarding scanning specifications and metadata. Retain this documentation after a project is completed so that future collection managers may reference it.

Prioritize: Use your documented guidelines to prioritize potential projects in a systematic way, taking into consideration factors such as demand for the collection, its size, and available technical and human resources. Try to strike a balance between small projects that can be completed relatively quickly and large ones that may be ongoing for a prolonged period of time. Keep an updated list of projects along with their priority levels and your current progress on each one.

Track: In addition to tracking projects in the aggregate, develop a system for monitoring the individual stages of each project as they are completed. This is crucial for keeping track of projects that have multiple workers assigned to them, not simply for the sake of organization but also for quality control purposes. Your method may be as simple as creating a shared spreadsheet or Google Doc for each project which workers can use to record tasks as they are completed, or you may employ a more sophisticated tool such as a project management program. There are a variety of free applications available, including Trello (https://trello.com) and Asana (https://asana.com). These types of software are often designed for use by sizable organizations that have large groups of people working on a project, and therefore may prove too complex for a solo digital librarian's needs, but you may also find that they provide some useful features that you can harness to support your specific workflows.

ABILITY TO COLLABORATE

As you have seen, the solo digital librarian does not truly work alone, but relies on assistance from others to maintain a productive and successful digitization program. This assistance extends beyond the invaluable help of support staff who perform essential work like scanning, and includes the participation of professional colleagues both within and outside the institution. Digitization is a collaborative activity that benefits from the input of people with different areas of specialization, and as you begin your digitization program you will want to consult with relevant stakeholders at your institution, which may include archivists, curators, catalogers, subject specialists, administrators, web designers, and IT professionals. Their feedback will be required in matters of policy making, project planning, technology, funding, and staffing. An important part of your job will be to act as an intermediary and catalyst, facilitating communication and collaboration between diverse parties. In this role, you will need to harness the expertise of individuals with various backgrounds and agendas and synthesize it with your own knowledge of digitization best practices.

In the earliest stages of developing your digitization program, you should identify a core group of stakeholders at your organization who will participate in planning and oversight of the program over time. At a large institution, this group may be made up mostly of staff within a single digital services department. At smaller institutions, it will likely require a greater degree of interdepartmental cooperation. If you are the sole digital librarian at your institution, then you will by necessity collaborate to some extent with colleagues from throughout the organization. An in-depth look at cross-departmental collaboration appears in chapter 3.

You may also find yourself collaborating with people outside of your organization, whether through membership in a consortium or simply an informal partnership with another institution. These types of relationships are very common in the cultural heritage community, and many digitization projects would not be feasible without a certain degree of inter-institutional cooperation. At its most basic, this may take the form of an arrangement to share digitization equipment for unusual scanning formats. More complex collaborations may result in combined digital collections featuring materials from multiple institutions. Strategies for working successfully in cross-institutional collaborations are examined in greater detail in chapter 4.

ABILITY TO NETWORK

Even if you aren't participating in any cross-institutional collaborative projects, as a solo digital librarian you will benefit greatly from cultivating relationships with colleagues at other institutions, for the simple reason that you will not know how to do everything yourself. You will at times need others to turn to who can answer questions and provide advice and guidance when you are uncertain about how to proceed with a particular matter. With enough research and trial and error you may be able to find your own answers to many problems, but it is often much more efficient and straightforward to simply speak with someone who has already resolved a specific issue and can give you advice on how to do so yourself. Most professionals in the cultural heritage community are more than happy to share their experiences and expertise with colleagues who may be struggling with a problem that they have already worked through.

In this way, there is a great deal of informal, ad hoc collaboration that occurs in the cultural heritage digitization community, and you can garner assistance from colleagues who you have never actually met in person and with whom you have no formal working relationship. As a solo digital librarian, you can save yourself much time and hand-wringing by tapping into the collective wisdom of this network of professionals. This can be accomplished by introducing yourself to colleagues at conferences and workshops; participating in conversations on e-mail lists, online discussion boards, and social media; and volunteering to serve with professional groups and organizations that focus on digitization-related activities. The larger your network, the greater the breadth of perspectives, approaches, and ideas you will have to draw on for your own work.

If you are just starting out as a solo digital librarian, you may also consider pursuing a formal or informal mentorship with a more experienced colleague in the field. This can be an invaluable way to receive individualized guidance and feedback as you navigate through your first digitization projects. Many professional organizations offer formal mentoring programs that allow those who are new to the profession, or just to a particular position, to be paired with experienced colleagues who are willing to engage in a structured advising relationship. An informal mentorship is generally instigated by the participants, and may be focused less on specific training and goals and more on providing the mentee an opportunity to receive help and encouragement. A good mentoring relationship offers more than learning skills for a job; it provides support for both professional and personal questions (Zanin-Yost 2013). This can be especially beneficial for the professional who may feel isolated by a lack of colleagues at his or her institution who are engaged in similar types of work.

ABILITY TO COMMUNICATE AND ADVOCATE EFFECTIVELY

In a survey of digital librarians at thirty-nine academic and research libraries, participants were asked to rate the importance of various technology, library-related, and managerial competencies and knowledge in performing their work; the highest-ranked choice was communication and interpersonal skills (Choi and Rasmussen 2006). It is difficult to overestimate the significance of effective communication in the work of the digital librarian. As mentioned previously, people both within and outside your organization may have only a vague understanding of the work you are doing. If you are the only person doing this type of work at your institution, you will be responsible for communicating to others the scope and value of your work. Good communication is especially important when participating in collaborative relationships, which are often part and parcel of the solo digital librarian's job. These can involve partners from various backgrounds who may not easily speak each other's professional language, and who may have competing agendas and priorities. In these situations, clear communication can mean all the difference between a successful project and one that never gets off the ground.

Along with this, you will need to be able to advocate for your own needs within the institution. If you are the only person managing digitization projects at your organization, then you will be the de facto expert in your area, regardless of how confident you feel in your knowledge. Others, including administrators and supervisors, will look to you for guidance in matters in which they may have little expertise, for example in making decisions about hardware and software purchases and staffing to support digitization projects. Your honest input is crucial for ensuring that you have the tools you need to do your work efficiently and effectively. If your needs aren't being met, then the onus will be on you to communicate this and make a case for change. If you aren't sure what you need, then seek support in taking the necessary steps to gain this knowledge, whether that be funding for the purchase of learning materials like books or for attendance at workshops or conferences.

In terms of self-advocacy, you may also need to remind others in your organization to have realistic expectations about what you are able to accomplish as a solo digital librarian who is responsible for juggling many varied tasks. To reiterate a point made previously, you can only accomplish so much on your own. Without a clearly defined job description and expectations, solo practitioners will quickly find themselves overwhelmed—or worse, misunderstood and undervalued (Spencer 2012). While you may have support staff or volunteers to help you, you are still attempting to single-handedly accomplish a job that could easily be tackled by an entire department. Communicate with your supervisor to ensure that the demands being made of you are reasonable and that your position is defined in such a way that it does not set you up for failure.

TROUBLESHOOTING TECHNOLOGY

As mentioned previously, dealing with problems and uncertainties related to technology is par for the course for the digitization professional. You will learn as you test out new things that there is a certain art to troubleshooting technology, which lies in harnessing the power of the Internet to piece together answers to your questions. You will have to become something of a detective to track down pertinent information. Especially when it comes to open source software, there is usually no tech support person available to assist you if a program doesn't behave correctly or you receive a cryptic error message on your screen (unless you are paying a third party to provide such support). Troubleshooting technology in these cases usually boils down to a process of elimination and a persistent trial-and-error approach.

One of the first places you should look for answers is in any product documentation provided by the vendor or software developer. Limited types of documentation, such as installation instructions, can typically be found within the root files of the software itself (usually with the file name READ ME). You'll most likely find the most complete information online, but this can be more of a challenge when dealing with noncommercial software. Widely used and well-established open source software products usually have a website or wiki containing documentation, although the comprehensiveness of this information can vary greatly. When evaluating open source software, it's a good idea to investigate the online community of users. Products that have a large and active user community will provide greater opportunities for assistance in the absence of the technical support that you would receive with a commercial product. Look for and browse user discussion forums, message boards, and e-mail lists that are specific to that product, and notice how quickly and thoroughly participants respond to each other's queries. In general, there are countless online communities that you can tap into for guidance, which is why the technology user community is often the best place to go for help. It is full of people who are experimenting and learning, just like you. Chances are good that someone has experienced a problem similar to yours, made an online appeal for help, and gotten answers from fellow users.

Another tip for troubleshooting technology on your own is to enter an error message verbatim into a search engine; if the error has been encountered by others (which it likely has) you may be able to locate discussions about it that will contain possible solutions or clues for further research. The hard part, of course, can be understanding the technical jargon that accompanies the information you find, which is often written for software developers or computer programmers. The art of troubleshooting is also an exercise in building your technological literacy—as you come across terminology you don't understand, you look it up, and slowly start to build a conceptual map of what the various pieces are and how they fit together. Again, this takes patience and persistence, but it is entirely possible for someone with little technology expertise to teach him or herself how to do things like compile and configure software or work with files in a command-line interface. Finally, be sure to keep track of and document your own troubleshooting process so you can refer back to the steps you've taken and the solutions you've found. Sometimes a seemingly unrelated issue can have a bearing on a future problem, and you will be glad you have notes to look back on to jog your memory.

Final Thoughts

If you are doing digital projects at a small or mid-sized institution, chances are good that you may be working more or less alone, managing projects and addressing technology issues without a lot of built-in support and input from colleagues. This can be viewed as both a challenge and an opportunity to be embraced. Solo digital librarianship can allow you a degree of creativity that is unparalleled in other areas within the cultural heritage community, providing the opportunity to shepherd a project through from conception to completion. The results of your efforts can be enormously satisfying.

As the saying goes, with freedom comes responsibility, and taking ownership of your institution's digitization efforts can be a formidable prospect. It's incumbent upon you to seek out allies both within and outside your institution, and to purposefully and strategically create your own community of support. A balance must be struck between taking charge and seeking help when appropriate and necessary, between being self-sufficient and recognizing and working around your own limitations. With these thoughts in mind, the following two chapters will take a more in-depth look at the importance of collaboration in digitization.

RECOMMENDED RESOURCES

BloggERS! (https://saaers.wordpress.com/)—blog of the Electronic Resources Section of the Society of American Archivists that covers topics in electronic records management and digital archives, including issues, case studies, how-tos, and tools.

Code4Lib Journal (http://journal.code4lib.org)—online, open-access journal focusing on the intersections of libraries and technology.

Computers in Libraries (www.infotoday.com/cilmag/)—subscription-based magazine covering news and issues in the field of library information technology.

D-Lib Magazine (www.dlib.org/)—free, online periodical covering digital library research and development.

Digital Preservation Matters (http://preservationmatters.blogspot.com/)—the personal blog of Chris Erickson, digital preservation officer at Brigham Young University Libraries, who writes about digital preservation, archiving, and curation.

Digitization 101 (http://hurstassociates.blogspot.com/)—blog of librarian and digitization consultant Jill Hurst-Wahl, who has been writing about digitization since 2004.

The Signal (http://blogs.loc.gov/thesignal/)—blog published by the Library of Congress that looks at issues and news related to digital preservation and access.

Webopedia (www.webopedia.com/)—online computer technology dictionary that provides easy-to-understand definitions for users with a wide range of computer knowledge.

REFERENCES

Choi, Youngok, and Edie Rasmussen. 2006. "What Is Needed to Educate Future Digital Librarians: A Study of Current Practice and Staffing Patterns in Academic and Research Libraries." *D-Lib Magazine* 12, no. 9 (September). doi: 10.1045/september 2006-choi.

LeFurgy, Bill. 2011. "What Skills Does a Digital Librarian or Archivist Need?" *The Signal*. Blog post, July 13. http://blogs.loc.gov/digitalpreservation/2011/07/what-skills-does-a-digital-archivist-or-librarian-need.

McGlone, Jonathan. 2013. "Looking under the Hood: A View of the Digital Projects Librarian in an Academic Library." In *The New Academic Librarian: Essays on Changing Roles and Responsibilities,* edited by Rebecca Peacock and Jill Wurm, 67–88. Jefferson, NC: McFarland.

Spencer, Roxanne Myers. 2012. "Solo Librarians as Jugglers." In *How to Thrive as a Solo Librarian,* edited by Carol Smallwood and Melissa J. Clapp, 3–12. Lanham, MD: Scarecrow.

Zanin-Yost, Alessia. 2013. "Mentoring: Planting the Seeds for Learning and Growing in the Library Profession." In *Continuing Education for Librarians,* edited by Carol Smallwood, Kerol Harrod, and Vera Gubnitskaia, 164–71. Jefferson, NC: McFarland.

WORKING ACROSS DEPARTMENTS

AS DISCUSSED IN CHAPTER 2, DIGITIZATION PROFESSIONals don't work in a vacuum—there is typically a certain amount of collaboration required to successfully carry out a digitization program. This may translate into a simple arrangement to borrow materials for reformatting, or it may take the form of a complex set of workflows involving the contributions of numerous stakeholders. This is true regardless of whether you are working as a solo digital librarian or as part of a digitization department or unit. You may start out with the objective of being autonomous in your work, and indeed, as Gueguen and Hanlon assert, "librarianship, and certainly curatorship, does not naturally gravitate toward ceding control over any aspect of collections" (2009). But if you ever intend to expand the scope of your digital collection building efforts, you will need to consider bringing in contributors from other parts of your organization to create a more efficient path toward this goal.

A 2006 survey of academic libraries engaged in efforts to digitize locally owned, print-based content found that fully 84 percent used crossdepartmental project groups to handle aspects of digitization at their libraries, and half involved other academic units on their campuses (Boock and

Vondracek 2006). If anything, these numbers have likely risen in the intervening years as digitization has become more of a core function of many organizations. The study illustrates that a robust and effective digitization program is usually a team effort that may cross traditional boundaries both within and beyond institutional walls.

This chapter will focus on collaborations that occur within an institution, involving people from multiple organizational units. It includes an examination of possible interdepartmental workflows and best practices for managing support staff, students, and volunteers. While it's true that the more participants you involve in a project, the more complicated it can become, once you have found a management method that works for you the benefits of collaboration will generally outweigh any difficulties. At the same time, there is often a tipping point beyond which the involvement of additional people in a project is liable to have the effect of slowing progress rather than advancing it. With experience, you will learn to strike a balance in this regard and get a sense for the optimal number of participants needed to make an individual partnership successful.

Potential Collaborators

The list of potential digitization collaborators to be found within a cultural heritage institution can encompass personnel from virtually all departments. Specialists from almost any area within a library, archive, or museum can have something to contribute to the process of building digital collections. The roles that different participants play will depend on the organizational structure and culture of your particular institution—for example, for one library it may make sense for scanning to occur in a technical services department, and for another in the archives; yet another may conduct this activity in both units at once. The following are possible functions that various institutional stakeholders may undertake in the digitization process.

Archives/Special Collections/Curatorial: Professionals within these units tend to be the caretakers of physical materials to be digitized, and as such their cooperation and involvement in digitization projects is crucial. At many institutions, particularly smaller ones, they often play a central role in digitization and may take charge of much of the process, while at others they may be more peripheral and act simply as gatekeepers to content. If you are not yourself an archivist, special collections librarian, or curator, the chances are great that you will at least work with one to gain access to the materials that you would like to reformat. He or she can provide valuable input for materials selection and prioritization, advising on the suitability of an item or collection for digitization based on such factors as physical condition, cultural or historical value, and anticipated demand from patrons.

Technical Services: Within libraries, the technical services or cataloging division can be a highly valuable partner in digital collection building. The technical services professional with a background in original cataloging is an obvious choice to engage in metadata-related work, and support staff who perform copy cataloging are often also well-equipped to assist in this regard. Due to their knowledge of cataloging rules, standards, and controlled vocabularies, technical services professionals can play an indispensable role in both the planning and execution of digitization projects.

Web Services/Graphic Design: These days, it's not uncommon for even small cultural heritage institutions to have a person on staff who specializes in web design, and at larger institutions there may be a web services department tasked with managing the organization's overall online presence. It makes sense that these professionals would have expertise to offer in planning and managing the delivery of digital collections. They may be involved in evaluating possible DCMSs to be used for displaying digitized materials, and they may implement interface design customizations to a system once it is selected. Colleagues in web services may also offer helpful insight into usability issues that can improve the user experience for patrons as they interact with online collections. Graphic designers, who may be more likely to be found in a museum setting rather than at a library or archive, may also be able to provide services related to interface design and website branding.

Systems: If you work at a large enough institution, most likely a library, you may have a systems department that administers, supports, and maintains technology services and systems, including hardware, software, and networking. Or there may be a single person within another unit, such as technical services, that specializes in this work. The obvious overlap between systems and digitization is in the oversight of your DCMS and general file management. If you are implementing a locally installed instance of an open source system, the systems librarian can play a key role in implementing, customizing, and troubleshooting the software. He or she may operate the servers where the software is installed and your digital files are stored, backed up, and preserved. Systems librarians may also work to integrate the DCMS with other products employed by the organization, such as online catalogs, discovery layers, or authentication systems.

Information Technology (IT): Cultural heritage institutions of all sizes generally have some type of IT presence, whether in the form of an internal or external department or a single support professional. The role of the IT professional is closely aligned with that of the systems librarian, and in relation to your digitization program he or she may perform a very similar function of administering the technical aspects of your DCMS, including installation, configuration, troubleshooting, and server management, as well as providing storage and backup for your digital files. Where IT professionals and systems librarians typically differ is in their level of specialized knowledge of information systems and practices, with the latter often having a greater understanding of the actual functionalities afforded by a DCMS and how they will be used. IT professionals commonly have a strong mandate for ensuring cyber security, so you will likely engage with them to ensure that your online collections are adequately protected and that the software meets institutional standards for online security. Unfortunately, this focus on system security can sometimes be at odds with the use of open source systems and the cultural heritage community's emphasis on open access to information.

Electronic Resources: If you work in a library, you may have one or more colleagues with the title of electronic resource librarian. These professionals are generally charged with acquiring and managing electronic subscription resources such as journals, databases, and e-books, so they are familiar with the delivery of collections of digital content online. If you choose to license a commercial DCMS that is hosted by a vendor, an electronic resource librarian can provide valuable assistance with licensing issues and vendor relations. He or she is also usually skilled at obtaining, compiling, and analyzing use data, and this can be helpful in assessing the use and impact of your digital collections once they are online.

Collection Development: Collection development professionals in libraries are tasked with developing and managing library collections, and this expertise can be leveraged for the development of digital collections as well. They may collaborate with archivists or special collections managers to select materials for digitization that comply with the institution's overall collection development priorities, or they may provide input into the formulation of a development policy expressly created for digital collections. In academic libraries, subject liaisons or bibliographers often have collection development responsibilities and possess specialized knowledge of discipline-specific resources as well as the needs and interests of faculty in their assigned areas, and they can bring this understanding to bear on material selection and collection planning. They may also utilize their faculty connections to recruit participation from campus stakeholders and promote digital collections to the larger institutional community.

Preservation/Conservation: Many cultural heritage institutions employ professionals as preservationists or conservators, and these people can play a role in the selection and preparation of materials for digitization. Some fragile materials are not suitable for digitization or need special handling to undergo the process without incurring further damage; your colleagues in preservation and conservation can evaluate potential materials for digitization, assess their physical state, and recommend approaches for protecting them during reformatting. They may apply measures such as disbinding, loosening pages, cleaning, or other forms of restoration or stabilization prior to digitization procedures. At some institutions the actual act of digital reformatting may take place within a preservation or conservation unit so that the materials can be closely monitored during the process.

Administration: Library and archives administrators and museum directors have a crucial part to play in the development of their institution's digitization programs by providing general guidance and support for those who are conducting digitization activities. They may not be directly involved in the collection building process, but they are typically instrumental in laying the groundwork that allows these activities to happen, including securing funding for equipment and personnel, weighing in on policies and procedures, and providing general oversight of the scope and direction of the program. They can make connections and negotiate partnerships with stakeholders both inside and outside the institution who may have materials to digitize, or some other type of expertise to lend. Administrators can also be important advocates of your institution's digitization efforts, communicating the significance of this work to institutional colleagues and the public at large. Even though they likely aren't engaged in day-to-day digitization activities, administrators are nonetheless valuable partners in the higher-level management and planning aspects of digitization.

Public Relations/Development: Public relations personnel can provide a vital service during the final stages of the digitization process, once a collection has been completed and made available online. All the work involved in designing and building a digital collection is in many ways wasted if the materials aren't utilized, so an essential step in the project workflow is to publicize the final product to its intended audience, whether that be students, scholars, or the general public. If your institution employs a public relations officer or team, they can utilize their marketing expertise and connections with the media to help expose potential users to digital collections that may be of interest to them. Similarly, development professionals may work to promote an institution's newsworthy projects and events with the aim of fostering support from alumni, donors, volunteers, and the public. If you have either of these types of colleagues at your organization, it is worth making an effort to keep them apprised of milestones such as the launch of a new digital collection so they can work with you to get the word out about your accomplishments.

Instruction/Public Services/Education: Colleagues at your organization may engage in structured educational activities, and they can also contribute to the promotion of your digital collections. At an academic library, instruction librarians educate students about the information resources available to them and provide training in how to use these resources; they may be able to incorporate your digital collections into their curricula as a way of introducing the materials to students and encouraging their use. Instruction librarians may also be in a position to provide input into digital collection planning with an eye toward integrating the materials into coursework. Cultural heritage institutions that are oriented more toward serving the general public, such as public libraries and museums, will often offer educational programming for visitors and patrons in the form of lectures, workshops, and the like. Public services librarians and museum educators who engage in these types of outreach activities are likewise in a good position to share digital collections with the public, as well as to provide insight to collection developers about how digital collections can be designed to best serve the needs of users.

Interdepartmental Workflows

As the previous section clearly demonstrates, the possibilities for interdepartmental collaboration are wide-ranging. Nearly everyone at your institution has a potential role to play in your digital collections program, from the central to the peripheral. However, this doesn't mean that it is appropriate or desirable to involve all these players in the digitization process at your specific institution, or that particular units must perform certain prescribed tasks as described above. The optimal system for managing and executing digital projects is entirely dependent on the unique structure and culture of each institution, and the most viable strategy usually relies upon leveraging an organization's existing strengths. The knowledge and expertise of specific staff members will help determine which units should be involved—for example, at one institution there may be personnel in the archives who have experience using a certain metadata schema, while at another institution this skill may be held by someone in a technical services or cataloging department. The following section will explore possible configurations and highlight successful interdepartmental arrangements that have been implemented by various organizations. The cases studied are taken from the academic library community, but the organizational strategies they illustrate can be applied to other settings such as archives, museums, and historical societies.

As mentioned earlier, archives and special collections staff are often central figures in the digitization process. If they do not manage the digitization process within their own division, they will frequently work in close partnership with digital librarians and other digitization specialists to do so cross-departmentally. Boock, Jeppesen, and Barrow (2002) describe how digitization efforts at the Cleveland State University Library, a medium-sized academic library, originated solely within the Special Collections Department, which consisted of one librarian and several students. As the program grew in scale it expanded to become an interdepartmental collaboration with the Technical Services, Systems, and Collection Development departments. The heads of these departments formed a committee that was tasked with selecting a new DCMS, and responsibilities for ensuing projects were broken down in the following manner:

- Special Collections provided the historical materials to be digitized and set the overall priority for projects;
- Technical Services managed digital production work such as scanning, storing, and preserving digital images, and developed cataloging rules and metadata schema for specific digital collections;
- Collection Development provided general supervision of digitization

projects, selection of images to be digitized, liaison work with faculty, cataloging of images, and promotion of collections;
- Systems selected, installed, and supported scanning hardware and software and a server to run the DCMS software, as well as designing web pages for the individual collections within the DCMS.

According to the authors, the key to success in this collaborative arrangement was identifying appropriate staff based on their existing skills, proving that "good things could be accomplished if the right people were involved and they were asked to do what they knew best" (ibid. 2002).

In the case of Cleveland State University, most of the departments involved reported to the same supervisor, the head of collection management. However, coordinating workflows between units with different reporting channels can prove to be more complex and require greater formalization of processes and procedures. At another midsized academic library, the University of Houston Libraries, digitization projects were developed jointly between three departments, Digital Services, Web Services, and Special Collections, all of which reported to different administrators (Prilop, Westbrook, and German 2012). Like Cleveland State, this collaborative structure also arose out of initial digitization efforts that were localized solely in Special Collections, and expanded to include other departments as the scale of the digitization program grew. The three departments shared equally in project leadership, and the resulting processes and procedures required thoughtful planning and documentation including graphical representations of workflows, implementation time lines, and the creation of an automated workflow and materials tracking system.

Rather than create entirely new systems for streamlining digitization programs, it is often easier to harness existing workflows. When the University of Maryland Libraries first developed its digital repository, an effort was made to capture digitization that was already being done in response to patron requests (Gueguen and Hanlon 2009). A newly created Office of Digital Collections and Research was responsible for coordinating digital initiatives and managing the digital repository, and content for the repository was gathered from the Department of Archives and Manuscripts and other units, which had been scanning materials for patron requests for some time. This "neutral collection-building" model effectively eliminated the need for purposeful content selection, thus creating efficiencies in the workflow that allowed for increased production. Obviously, this method is not suitable for "boutique" or exhibit-style digital collections that require careful curation. But it does illustrate the concept that existing resources can be adapted for the purposes of streamlining and expanding the digital collection building process.

Similarly, cross-training between departments can be a low-cost way to expand your digitization program by taking advantage of existing staff competencies. At the University of Denver's Penrose Library, a consolidated cataloging and archives unit was created that combined staff from the Special Collections and Archives unit and the Technical Services unit, thus allowing metadata creation and management for digital collections to be integrated into the overall materials processing workflow (Colati, Crowe, and Meagher 2009). In order to combine the units and merge workflows, monograph and serials catalogers from Technical Services were trained in archival theory, practice, and processing. This training, combined with the catalogers' traditional background in item-level bibliographic control, "uniquely placed [them] to step into key roles in digital library projects" by contributing high-quality metadata for digital objects in a way that archival staff, who were versed mainly in collection-level description, could not.

Many institutions have found that repurposing existing staff for digitization projects provides value for partnering units that may be experiencing declines in their traditional workloads. A common example of this is in libraries, where increased purchasing of nonprint formats and electronic resource packages has resulted in reduced activity in traditional areas such as receiving, processing, invoicing, and cataloging. Taking advantage of this freed-up staff time can be a key step in scaling up digitization efforts, as librarians at Eastern Illinois University's Booth Library found. They were able to dramatically increase digital production by reassigning staff from the Circulation Department, which was experiencing diminishing amounts of work, to a newly created scanning center for digital projects (Bruns et al. 2014). Reassigned staff from Circulation and the library's Technology Services Department were tasked with supervising student scanning staff in the center.

Beyond the apparent partnerships which have been mentioned previously, there can also be opportunities for less obvious collaborators to participate in digitization projects. For example, at Oregon State University Libraries, the Interlibrary Loan (ILL) Department possessed a planetary (overhead) book scanner that it shared with the Digital Production unit, which did not have a scanner suitable for efficiently reformatting bound books (Kunda 2010). For digitization projects involving monographs, the two units worked out a schedule that allowed ILL students to digitize books using the planetary scanner during hours when it was not being heavily used for ILL requests. ILL was one player in a collaboration that also involved the Cataloging, Archives, and Special Collections departments. In addition, subject librarians were enlisted in certain cases to assist with collection development, assessing materials in their area of specialization to determine if they were possible candidates for digitization.

Best Practices for Collaborative Project Management

Clearly, there are a variety of ways that collaborative digitization projects can be organized within a given institution, and the cases described above provide just a few examples. Because of this diversity, there is not necessarily a general-purpose management approach that can be applied to all projects. But regardless of who is involved and how workflows are structured, there are certain methods and techniques that can encourage a smooth experience for all parties involved. This section offers guidelines for effectively developing and executing collaborative projects of all types and configurations.

PREPLANNING

The preplanning stage is an important aspect of project management in general, and it is especially critical for collaborative projects. Prior to embarking on a cross-departmental digitization project, there are certain preliminary steps that can help set a partnership up for success. A key activity is gaining buy-in from potential stakeholders and participants. Cervone defines obtaining buy-in as "getting the right message to the right people in the right way" (2005). You may need to tailor your communication to various partners in order to address their individual concerns; this can help ensure their consistent support throughout the life cycle of the project or program. True buy-in entails more than merely securing an agreement to share in the work; it requires a common understanding and vision to guide and engage participants for the long term. For those colleagues who are not normally involved in digitization activities, the benefits of a digitization program may not be well understood.

Efforts to inspire interest and educate potential partners in this regard can contribute significantly to a project's future success. Lampert and Vaughan outline some approaches for promoting staff buy-in, including conducting informational workshops and integrating digital collection building into the institution's overall strategic plan and individual department goals (2009).

Additionally, it helps to have a well-thought-out and clearly articulated plan of action prior to approaching digitization partners. Prilop, Westbrook, and German gave a formal presentation of a proposed digitization workflow to stakeholders at their institution, and anticipated in advance potential questions and issues that might be raised by attendees (2012). Soliciting feedback and suggestions from stakeholders, including students and staff who will be responsible for completing the work, can also help encourage a sense of investment in the project and provide a means for identifying more efficient workflows.

Once you have buy-in from stakeholders and a tentative plan in place, it may also be a good idea to experiment with potential workflows before committing to a particular one. Kunda recommends devising multiple possible workflows and testing them out in their entirety to find the best one before formally starting a project (2010). This step can save time down the road because it is easier to make changes to a workflow in the beginning stages of a project. Having a good understanding of different departments' existing workflows can also make the process of designing an appropriate collaborative workflow more efficient and straightforward.

COMMUNICATION
The success of a cross-departmental digitization project or program hinges on many factors, but it may be argued that none is as crucial as good communication among participants. These types of partnerships often bring together individuals and parties who are not accustomed to working closely together, and this dynamic can lead to miscommunication and conflict if not handled thoughtfully. The "meeting of the minds" that collaboration entails can lead to greater progress and efficiency, encouraging new ideas and enhanced problem-solving, or it may result in confusion, disorganization, and gridlock. Practices that encourage clear and continuing communication should be established during the preplanning stages and maintained throughout a project's life cycle to ensure that channels of communication remain open.

A first step in fostering transparency is to clearly define and document policies and procedures. This may include mission statements, selection criteria, scanning specifications, metadata guidelines, and documentation that tracks project priorities, time lines, and workflows. These records can help guide project staff in their work and support managers in their decision-making, but they are only effective if they are utilized. It's important to make this information readily available to project participants and make sure that it is clearly understood. Unfortunately, it is not uncommon for project managers to spend countless hours crafting documentation that ends up languishing in a file folder, largely unread.

To create a culture of good communication among project team members, an essential component of your management strategy should be to schedule regular meetings for project leaders. If you have a committee tasked with overseeing digital projects or programs, arrange to have the group meet on a recurring basis for purposes of planning, troubleshooting, and reviewing and updating procedures. As Kunda points out, conducting periodic "check-ins" is important for maintaining consistency (2010). Regular check-ins between project managers and staff or volunteers who are doing production work may also be necessary, especially during the beginning stages of a project, to ensure that procedures are clearly understood and quality benchmarks are being met. In general, regularly scheduled discussions also serve to encourage accountability from project partners at all levels, which can be difficult to maintain in situations where participants may have different reporting channels. When a project or program has reached a stage in which the workflow is smooth and predictable, a more ad hoc approach may be taken, with check-ins scheduled only as needed.

One of the more challenging aspects of collaborative digitization is often related to decision-making and reaching consensus about issues such as project selection and prioritization. Group members from different organizational units may have competing viewpoints about the relative importance of certain aspects of a project, or have varying levels of risk aversion when it comes to concerns like copyright. Good communication is imperative for managing the decision-making process in diverse teams so that all members feel heard and understood. The process should take into account the interest of all affected parties, as well as clarifying and defining the real objectives of the situation, which can often be difficult to tease out (Cervone 2005). It's important to involve all stakeholders in the decision-making process to the maximum extent possible, and to ensure that decisions made are communicated and made understandable to those outside the team.

EVALUATION

When decisions are made and procedures implemented, it does not signify the end of the project process. An important aspect of collaborative digitization management is conducting recurring evaluations of workflows, with review of procedures being made a continuous part of the project life cycle. This is a large part of the reason why it is essential to conduct regular check-ins or meetings, as they provide a natural and spontaneous opportunity for project assessment. You may also wish to carry out more formal evaluations at key points during the project life cycle, such as at midterm and completion. Areas to assess for each project may include the following:

- Are guidelines and specifications being accurately followed?
- Are measures of quality being successfully met?
- Are established workflows efficient and smooth, or do bottlenecks occur at certain points?
- Are improvements needed in training or communication methods?
- Are procedures adequately documented?

In addition to project-level evaluation, collaborators should periodically review the effectiveness of the digitization program as a whole. This activity is especially important as the scale of the program expands, and in cases where new participants may be brought on board. Workflows that function well for small projects may prove inefficient for larger ones, and processes may need to be streamlined in order to maintain an acceptable level of productivity. For example, as their digitization programs scale up, it is not uncommon for institutions to streamline their metadata practices by placing less emphasis on detailed description so that items may be processed more quickly. This mirrors closely the "more product, less process" philosophy embraced by some in the archives community, which advocates minimal processing as a means of eliminating backlogs and maximizing access to materials. You may find that other strategies are needed for dealing with backlogs in your own workflows, including training new staff members or volunteers and reassigning existing ones to take on new duties.

Above all, aim to maintain an attitude of flexibility, and encourage this approach among project collaborators. Realize that policies and procedures may not translate directly from one project to another, and be willing to make adjustments when needed. Integrating workflow evaluation and assessment into the digital project life cycle will make it easier for you and your partners to identify and correct issues before they become problems that may require significant backtracking or duplication of effort.

Final Thoughts

At many cultural heritage institutions, there is a natural evolution in the development of digitization activities and programs. Often they will begin as small, one-off projects that are executed by staff within a single unit, such as an archives or special collections department within a library. Over time, as the digitization program grows and more and larger collections are produced, the increased scale demands that a collaborative approach be adopted within the organization. Existing workflows in various departments are harnessed to maximize efficiency as digitization becomes woven more thoroughly into the overall institutional fabric. Ultimately, the creation and sharing of digital collections progresses from a series of discrete projects to a core service of the institution.

As you dip your toes in the digitization waters and embark on your first collections, it may seem difficult to see yourself that far along the path, or perhaps your institution is so small that there doesn't appear to be room for growth beyond a single-unit workflow. But even in the early stages of your digitization program, when it makes sense to start small, it also pays to start strategizing for possible future expansion. Laying the groundwork early on, by including others at your institution in the digitization conversation, will position you well for future developments and collaborative opportunities that may not be apparent to you at the present time.

REFERENCES

Boock, Michael, Bruce Jeppesen, and William Barrow. 2002. "Getting Digitization Projects Done in a Medium-Sized Academic Library: A Collaborative Effort between Technical Services, Systems, Special Collections, and Collection Management." *Technical Services Quarterly* 20, no. 19: 31. doi: 10.1300/J124v20n03_02.

Boock, Michael, and Ruth Vondracek. 2006. "Organizing for Digitization: A Survey." *portal: Libraries and the Academy* 6, no. 2: 192–217. doi: 10.1353/pla.2006.0015.

Bruns, Todd, Stacey Knight-Davis, Ellen K. Corrigan, and J. Steve Brantley. 2014. "It Takes a Library: Growing a Robust Institutional Repository in Two Years." *College and Undergraduate Libraries* 21, no. 3/4: 244-62. doi: 10.1080/10691316.2014.904207.

Cervone, H. Frank. 2005. "Making Decisions: Methods for Digital Library Project Teams." *OCLC Systems & Services: International Digital Library Perspectives* 21, no. 1: 30–35.

Colati, Gregory C., Katherine M. Crowe, and Elizabeth S. Meagher. 2009. "Better, Faster, Stronger: Integrating Archives Processing and Technical Services." *Library Resources and Technical Services* 53, no. 4: 261–70. www.ala.org/alcts/sites/ala.org.alcts/files/content/resources/lrts/archive/53n4.pdf.

Gueguen, Gretchen, and Ann M. Hanlon. 2009. "A Collaborative Workflow for the Digitization of Unique Materials." *The Journal of Academic Librarianship* 35, no. 5: 468–74. doi: 10.1016/j.acalib.2009.06.001.

Kunda, Sue. 2010. "Collaborating for Success: A Cross-Departmental Digitization Project." In *Digitization in the Real World: Lessons Learned from Small and Medium-Sized Digitization Projects,* edited by Kwong Bor Ng and Jason Kucsma, 541–55. New York: Metropolitan New York Library Council.

Lampert, Corey, and Jason Vaughan. 2009. "Success Factors and Strategic Planning: Rebuilding an Academic Library Digitization Program." *Information Technology and Libraries* 28, no. 3: 116–36. doi: 10.6017/ital.v28i3.3220.

Prilop, Valerie, R. Niccole Westbrook, and Elizabeth M. German. 2012. "Collaborative Project Development in the Creation of an Interdepartmental Digitization Workflow." *Collaborative Librarianship* 4, no. 2: 60–66.

WORKING ACROSS INSTITUTIONS

FOR CENTURIES, LIBRARIANS AND SCHOLARS ALIKE HAVE BEEN enticed by the idea of a universal library that contains all the world's knowledge. The legendary Great Library of Alexandria in ancient Egypt is thought to have approached this achievement, having been estimated to house between 30 and 70 percent of all books in existence at the time (Kelly 2006). Although the Library of Alexandria is long gone, the myth of the universal library maintains its hold on the cultural imagination in works of modern fiction such as Jorge Luis Borges's short story "The Library of Babel," which takes the concept a step further by envisioning a library that holds not only every existing book, but every possible one as well—a glut of random information that renders the knowledge contained within the library virtually useless. Borges's library can be likened to the Internet, which offers the promise of universal knowledge and yet suffers from its sheer size and chaotic disorganization.

Though a true universal library would be impossible to create or sustain, the advent of the Internet has made the ideal of universal knowledge more viable than ever before by making it possible to collect and aggregate digital content from disparate sources. Cultural heritage institutions have been at the forefront of efforts to harness digital technology with this goal in mind.

Initially, digitization projects at individual institutions resulted in self-contained "silos" of content, with digital collections isolated from each other in much the same way that their physical counterparts would be separated by library, archive, or museum walls. Many digitization initiatives now strive to break down these barriers, crossing institutional boundaries to create new collections from materials that were formerly unconnected. These initiatives require cross-institutional cooperation and collaboration on a scale larger than the interdepartmental arrangements described in chapter 3. The size and complexity of these types of collaborations can vary widely, ranging from two local institutions cooperating on a single digital project, to state or regional consortia aggregating digital collections from member institutions, and on to national and even international initiatives that come closer than ever before to embodying the archetype of the universal library.

In this chapter, we will examine the various types of inter-institutional digitization collaborations that are common in the cultural heritage community today. These arrangements can prove extremely beneficial for small and medium-sized institutions by allowing them to share resources and expertise with other organizations. For small cultural heritage institutions that lack adequate funding or personnel, participating in collaborative arrangements with outside entities can be the best way to get a digitization program off the ground. If your institution falls into this category, this chapter will provide you with strategies for taking advantage of the possibilities that collaborative digitization can provide.

Collaborative Mass Digitization Projects

Collaborative digitization on a large scale is most often associated with efforts to mass digitize books, and these initiatives have entered the cultural consciousness with various projects that have received significant media attention in recent years. As Coyle points out, mass digitization is more than just a large-scale project; it is the conversion of materials on an industrial scale without making a selection of individual items (2006). This is very different from the discrete digital collections that most individual institutions create, and which are the general focus of this book. Mass digitization generally involves minimal collection development, and has the goal of converting large amounts of materials as efficiently as possible. Even the largest libraries, archives, and museums often do not have the resources to do this type of work on their own, as it requires significant investments in equipment and personnel. A common model is for cultural heritage institutions to team up with well-funded commercial or nonprofit organizations that provide technology and manpower in exchange for access to materials and the right to make the resulting scans part of a searchable database.

Arguably the best-known, and most ambitious, mass digitization initiative is the Google Books project. Google publicly launched this program in 2004 with the stated goal of scanning all of the world's books and making them available online. As part of the project, Google has partnered with major academic, national, and public libraries from around the world, with initial membership including Harvard University, the University of Michigan, the New York Public Library, the University of Oxford, and Stanford University. In return for the physical act of scanning the books using its high-speed scanners, Google shares copies of the resulting digital files with the lending institutions. The list of institutional partners has since grown to over twenty, and as of September 2015, the number of scanned titles had reportedly reached thirty million (Wu 2015).

Because Google scans titles that are under copyright protection as well as those that are out of copyright (although the Google Books database only allows users to view "snippets" of protected works and not the full text), the project has been plagued by opposition from authors and publishers claiming copyright infringement. After years of litigation, the matter was seemingly settled in April 2016, when the U.S. Supreme Court declined to hear an appeal of the case *Authors Guild v. Google,* in which a lower court had ruled that Google's practice of digitizing for the purpose of indexing did not violate copyright law. While the Google Books project continues, it has not been fully embraced by some in the cultural heritage community who do not trust an individual commercial, for-profit entity with stewardship over such a large portion of the cultural record, fearing the possible privatization of public knowledge.

However, there are noncommercial alternatives to the Google Books project. Other collaborative mass digitization efforts have been undertaken by groups that are committed to full, permanent public access to digitized texts. For example, in 2005 the Open Content Alliance (OCA) was formed, in part as a response to Google Books. The OCA bills itself as "a collaborative effort of a group of cultural, technology, nonprofit, and governmental organizations from around the world that helps build a permanent archive of multilingual digitized text and multimedia materials" (www.opencontentalliance.org/about). The list of contributing institutions—those that have donated collections, services, tools, or funding to the initiative—includes large technology companies like Yahoo! and Adobe Systems, national and university libraries and regional library consortia, major museums like the Smithsonian and the American Museum of Natural History, and international organizations like the British Library and the National Library of Australia, as well as smaller organizations like county public libraries and historical societies. The OCA sets itself apart from Google Books in a variety of ways, most notably in its "opt-in" policy of obtaining permission from content owners before digitizing copyrighted materials (this is in contrast with Google's "opt-out" policy of digitizing copyrighted works unless explicitly told not to do so). While the total number of texts digitized is therefore much smaller, the OCA is able to make all of its materials fully available to users for download and reuse without restrictions. Unlike Google, the OCA also stores its materials in multiple institutional archives around the world in an effort to ensure transparency, accessibility, and long-term preservation.

The OCA contributes its digitized materials to the Internet Archive, which oversees one of the world's largest mass digitization endeavors. This nonprofit organization was founded in 1996 by Brewster Kahle, whose stated mission is universal access to all knowledge—making "the dream of the Library of Alexandria a reality" (Kahle 2007). In addition to books that are no longer under copyright, the Internet Archive provides free public access to websites, software, movies, and music. The Internet Archive administers scanning for the OCA at its international scanning centers as well as providing file storage and making the content accessible through its website, https://archive.org. Fittingly, the organization has its files backed up at the Bibliotheca Alexandrina in Egypt, a modern-day re-creation of the ancient Library of Alexandria built close to the original's location.

Large-Scale Collaborative Digital Repository Projects

While Google Books, the OCA, and the Internet Archive actively engage in materials scanning and reformatting to populate their digital repositories, there are also a number of initiatives that function as aggregators for digitized content that has been contributed by cultural heritage institutions. These projects focus primarily on providing long-term preservation and access services for institutions that have content that has been digitized in-house or through other means such as outsourcing. The goal of this category of large-scale collaborative project is to bring together digital content from disparate sources and provide a shared discovery interface. The following are examples of some of the largest and most high-profile collaborative digital repositories.

One of the most ambitious examples of this type of initiative is the Europeana platform (www.europeana.eu), which provides access to cultural heritage materials from partner institutions all over the European Union. This "meta-aggregator," launched in 2008, has grown to encompass over fifty million digital objects from 3,500 libraries, archives, and museums across Europe. In addition to texts, archival materials, and audio and video recordings, visual works of art are strongly represented, including iconic paintings from major international museums and galleries. The Europeana platform does not host the digitized objects themselves, but rather functions as a portal for accessing materials that are stored on partner institutions' networks. The repository "harvests" metadata records from partner institutions using the Open Archives Initiative Protocol for Metadata Harvesting (OAI-PMH), a set of communication rules for repository interoperability that allows for metadata sharing between systems. (According to the protocol, in this instance a partner organization functions as a "data provider" by exposing its metadata to the Europeana system, which acts as a "service provider" and harvests the metadata by issuing a set of OAI-PMH requests.) This data is then mapped to a standardized format known as the Europeana Data Model. This allows users to search across all records, preview an object, and download or view the original at the host website.

A similar project in the United States is the Digital Public Library of America, or DPLA (https://dp.la), a "national digital library" that seeks to organize and make accessible the content that cultural heritage institutions at the state, regional, and national levels have been digitizing for years. The web portal went online in 2013 and contains records for over thirteen million items. Like Europeana, the DPLA harvests metadata from existing digital collections into a single, searchable access point. Users who search the repository are directed to the contributing institutions' websites in order to retrieve the original digital files. To aggregate metadata from partner institutions, the DPLA utilizes a network model of "content hubs" and "service hubs." Content hubs are large institutions like the New York Public Library, the Smithsonian, and the Internet Archive that contribute their metadata records directly to the DPLA. Service hubs are collaborative groups at the state or regional level that serve as a point of contact for smaller partner institutions, collecting and enhancing their metadata before contributing it to the DPLA. The responsibilities of a service hub might be taken on by a regional or state consortium that has a collaborative digital repository service already in place, or a group of institutions such as state libraries, public libraries, universities, museums, archives, and historical societies may come together specifically to create a service hub.

A project that is larger in scope, but smaller in scale, is the World Digital Library, or WDL (www.wdl.org/en). This initiative was developed by the Library of Congress and is carried out with the support of the United Nations Educational, Cultural, and Scientific Organization (UNESCO). Partner organizations include libraries, archives, museums, and other cultural and educational institutions from around the world. The WDL focuses on providing access to "cultural treasures" from UNESCO member countries, which are nominated for inclusion by partner institutions and chosen by the WDL content selection committee in accordance with specific guidelines. Item-level descriptions are provided by curators and other experts who provide historical context and explain each object's significance. The time and resources devoted to collection development and resource description make the WDL unique among most large-scale collaborative projects. Because it is by comparison highly curated, it is therefore significantly smaller—as of this book's publication, it contained approximately 15,000 digital objects from around 200 institutions. The WDL also differs from other similar projects in that it is multilingual, giving users the ability to translate the site interface into seven different languages. Time lines, interactive maps, and in-depth exhibits on selected themes round out the value-added features that the site provides. Partner institutions may digitize their own content or utilize one of a number of digitization centers that have been established in developing countries.

Another large-scale, collaboratively sourced repository of note is the HathiTrust (www.hathitrust.org). While Europeana, DPLA, and WDL focus largely on enhancing accessibility to contributing institutions' content, the HathiTrust also has as its major goal the long-term preservation of materials that have been created via mass digitization initiatives like Google Books. *Hathi* is the Hindu word for elephant, an animal which, as the saying goes, never forgets. The HathiTrust was formed in 2008 by fourteen large research libraries in the United States, including a number of Google Books partner institutions, in reaction to concerns about the commitment of organizations like Google to ensure perpetual preservation of its digitized content over time. In addition to ensuring continuous preservation of massive digital library collections, the HathiTrust seeks to provide wide access to digital collections in a manner that is "unbeholden to commercial interests and in support of the activities of scholars" (Christenson 2011). Content in the repository, which ingests digital objects as well as their accompanying metadata, includes materials created as a result of Google Books' and the Internet Archive's scanning efforts, as well as locally digitized content from member libraries. In 2011 the HathiTrust was sued by the Authors' Guild for alleged massive copyright violation for including "unauthorized" books scanned by Google, but this case was dropped in 2015. The HathiTrust has grown to include over one hundred partner institutions from the United States and around the world, and as of June 2016 it comprised over fourteen million volumes (HathiTrust 2016).

State and Regional Collaborative Projects

For many small cultural heritage institutions, the most practical option for participating in a large-scale digital repository project is to partner with other organizations at the state or regional level. Often this takes the form of membership in a regional consortium or state-sponsored project that may offer resources ranging from digitization training and support to DCMS hosting and digital file storage. These types of arrangements can allow institutions that have no digitization program in place to get their content scanned and on the Web with relative ease and minimal outlays of time and money. They also offer an excellent option for institutions that have the means to digitize their own materials, but lack the technical infrastructure to make them easily accessible online—they may not be able to afford the cost of a commercial DCMS or have the ability to mount and run an open source platform. A consortial or regional digital library system can allow member institutions a cost-effective way to provide sophisticated user functionalities and widespread access to their digital content without the burden of maintaining servers, hardware, and software.

Even institutions that administer a dedicated local repository system for their digital content may find it beneficial to also contribute their materials to a state or regional collaborative project. Making content available through a central search portal, which most of these types of initiatives provide, can help make previously isolated content more widely discoverable online. Combining individual institutional holdings at a state or regional level can also create entirely new collections, breaking down institutional silo walls, creating connections between disparate collections, and providing users with new frameworks for viewing and interpreting materials. As the previous sections demonstrate with examples like Google Books and the HathiTrust, there is often overlap in the holdings of various collective digital repositories, and content need not be limited to a single access point.

As previously mentioned, content aggregation via a central search portal is often the main goal of collaborative projects at the state and regional levels. There are two common models for achieving this: partner institutions may upload their digital objects directly into a central repository platform, or they may make metadata that already exists for materials in their local DCMS available to be harvested into the central repository. The latter model generally does not require that partners contribute their actual digital objects; rather, users are redirected via a link back to the institutional site in order to view the original object. These metadata aggregators may be capable of searching a larger amount of content since they are storing metadata records and not digital files, which are typically quite large. However, they have the drawback of excluding participation from institutions that are not already hosting their own digital collections online.

Some collaborative projects, often those that are state- or grant-funded, focus more narrowly on serving institutions that do not have a way to digitize and provide access to their collections locally. They may offer digital conversion services for their partners at a centralized location like a state or university library. The downside to this arrangement is that it requires transporting physical materials outside the owning institution for conversion, which is often not ideal; however, with proper preparation and handling most materials will weather such a journey without incident. Generally, project administrators can assist partners in determining which of their materials are suitable for transport and which may be too fragile. For partner institutions that are expected to scan their own materials, instructions are generally provided outlining specifications that must be met in terms of file format and resolution.

There are variations on these two service models, such as the Mountain West Digital Library (MWDL), which employs something of a hybrid approach. The MWDL serves a large and varied membership, with over 180 partners from six western U.S. states, including libraries, archives, museums, historical societies, state agencies, and county and municipal governments. Perhaps due to its large size, the MWDL utilizes a "hub and spoke" service model that incorporates a regional network of hosting hubs offering digitization services and digital content hosting for surrounding institutions; content from the regional hubs is then aggregated into a central MWDL discovery portal (www.mwdl.org) via OAI-PMH metadata harvesting (Neatrour, Cummings, and McIntyre 2016). The MWDL itself also functions as a service hub for the DPLA.

In addition to providing assistance with digital format conversion and content aggregation, most collaborative digitization programs at the state and regional levels will provide some type of metadata support for contributing institutions. In cases where scanning is done as a service for partners or members, project staff may also create metadata to accompany the resulting digital files. In most cases, partner institutions are responsible for creating their own metadata, and will be provided with guidance for doing so in compliance with standards established by project administrators. This may take the form of workshops, training sessions, written standards documentation, or individualized feedback on metadata quality.

Another important benefit that these types of partnerships can offer is digital preservation services. For those participating in a model in which digital objects are uploaded to a central repository, this storage space can function as a geographically distributed backup solution. As discussed in chapter 9, this type of file backup is an important digital preservation strategy. It's crucial that institutions also store copies of their files locally because it is not good practice to have your institution's digital collections kept solely in a collaborative central repository. In cases where digital conversion is provided as a service, it's important to get copies of the files to be stored and managed long-term at your own institution as well.

While most collaborative arrangements have content aggregation as a core function, a less frequently seen type of service focuses mainly on DCMS hosting for member institutions. A consortium or other regional entity may provide individual instances of a repository platform that is collectively hosted and maintained at a central location. This may be done using a multi-site setup (one central repository installation that allows for multiple associated sites) or by creating separate repository installations for each site. Partners each have an individualized, custom DCMS for storing, managing, and delivering their digital collections, which may or may not feed into a shared discovery portal. This arrangement can be a good option for institutions that would like the autonomy of administering their own DCMS, but lack the resources to host and maintain the software on local servers. This type of software hosting is also commonly offered by third-party commercial vendors that specialize in open source repository systems.

Partnerships at the Local Level

Participation in large-scale partnerships at the state or regional level can sometimes spark local connections that lead to smaller-scale collaborations. For example, Middleton and Taylor describe how Middle Tennessee State University's (MTSU) involvement in the Tennessee statewide collaborative digitization project, Volunteer Voices (http://volunteervoices.org), led to further partnerships between the MTSU's Walker Library and other campus and community partners (2010). Based on knowledge and experience gained by building digital skills through the Volunteer Voices project, MTSU was able to develop its own locally hosted digital projects that featured materials from a county arts center, a prominent local family, a campus research center, and MTSU faculty members.

Local partnerships like these can originate in a variety of ways, and often arise from preexisting relationships between librarians, archivists, curators, educators, historians, and others who live and work in the same institution, town, or county. In contrast with the top-down, hierarchical structure of large-scale collaborative programs, these projects may be more grassroots and informal. Usually, an institution with an established digital infrastructure (often an academic library) will agree to digitize materials from an outside entity, whether that be a separate campus unit or an entirely different institution, which lacks the resources to do so itself. In this scenario the resulting files may be hosted by the digitizing institution in its local DCMS, so materials from lending institutions generally need to fall within the collecting scope of the larger digital library. A common theme of these types of partnerships is to bring together local history resources that reside in disparate locations.

Of course, there are myriad other possible variations on the local partnership arrangement. The cultural heritage community tends to be a collegial one, and the sharing of resources and expertise between institutions is generally supported and encouraged. You may have colleagues in neighboring institutions who would be willing, for example, to let you use their large-format scanner to digitize a set of oversize maps, or to give you advice on metadata creation or copyright issues. You may have the opportunity to pool resources for a shared DCMS, to collaborate on a grant to fund a digitization project, or to work jointly to recruit and organize volunteers to scan materials. When searching for collaborative opportunities at the local level, Raab suggests also reaching out to Friends' groups for assistance; exploring alternative funding sources (for example, if you are at an academic institution, you may consider approaching the presidents' or provosts' offices, alumni affairs, Greek organizations, athletics, facilities, or development); or creating a local digital cooperative (2007). It pays to be creative and flexible, to reach out to colleagues to identify common subject collections, and to make yourself available to assist others when possible. If you have a willingness to engage with others at the local level, you may find that a community partnership holds the key to moving your digitization projects forward.

Pros and Cons of Partnering outside Your Institution

For cultural heritage institutions that have small budgets and low levels of staffing, participation in a digitization partnership can offer many advantages. It can lower or eliminate start-up costs, which may be prohibitively expensive when hardware, software, and staff costs are factored in. While grant funding is often used to initiate a digitization program, this kind of support is invariably temporary. Collaboration can provide a more permanent solution for sustaining a cost-efficient digitization program over the long term.

In addition to lowering costs, collaborative digitization can ease the organizational burden for institutions that cannot or do not wish to manage their own digital collections infrastructure. Large-scale collaborative digitization projects at the national, state, or regional level offer a measure of convenience for small institutions because they are centrally managed by a third party, eliminating the need to maintain servers or software. Services for members usually include technological and administrative support, often with very basic assistance for partners that are new to digitization and need guidance in fundamental areas like scanning and metadata. A well-established collaborative program can provide its members directly with the tools and knowledge they need to successfully complete their first digitization projects, so they don't have to start from scratch.

Aside from these practical motivations, there are significant user-centered reasons why you may wish to contribute to a collaborative project like a large-scale digital library, even if you already host your own local digital collections. Making your unique materials accessible along with those from other institutions in a common discovery interface places your collections within the context of the larger cultural heritage community, and allows users to make new connections that may greatly enhance their research and scholarship. In a variety of ways, collaborative digitization can prove mutually beneficial for both institutions and their users.

Not surprisingly, there are certain disadvantages that may be associated with cross-institutional collaborations. As we have seen, while some large-scale digitization projects merely point to existing digital collections and do not collect the actual digitized materials, only the associated metadata, others require that participating institutions contribute copies of their image or audio/video files to the hosting organization. Some collections managers may balk at the prospect of giving up control of their materials in this way, fearing that it will open them up to misattribution or misuse. Cultural heritage professionals like archivists and curators, who are accustomed to having strict local control over physical materials in their care, may not feel comfortable giving a third party ownership of the digital surrogates. This anxiety arises most often in relation to partnerships with commercial entities such as Google, although it may also be enough of a concern to prevent some institutions from taking part in nonprofit or government-sponsored programs.

Another drawback that often comes with participation in collaborative projects, especially large ones, is that it imposes limits on the contributing institution's ability to dictate how materials are displayed and presented to users.

There is less creativity, flexibility, and choice involved in joining an existing project, with aspects like scanning specifications, DCMS platform, and metadata schema being generally predetermined by the larger partner organization. For participants at many small institutions this is an advantage, as it frees them from the burden of making such decisions. Often, it may be their only practical option for sharing their digital collections online, so the trade-off is worth it. But for those who have the option of creating their own digital library from scratch, it can be worth the extra work and expense involved in "going it alone" in order to maintain creative control over their digital collections.

Final Thoughts

As with many aspects of digital collection building, there is no "right" answer when it comes to the question of whether your institution would benefit from an outside collaboration. In many cases, but not necessarily all, the pros of such arrangements outweigh the cons, especially for small institutions. Collaborative digitization projects of all sizes have proven critical to the goal of making hidden collections more accessible, and have allowed entrée into the world of digitization for institutions that would otherwise not have the means to pursue such work. Since the burning of the ancient library in Alexandria, they also, perhaps, hold the most promise for making the ideal of the universal library a reality in modern times.

If you do choose to pursue partnerships outside your institution, it's important to keep in mind that collaboration doesn't have to be an either/or prospect. You can participate in multiple associations at different levels simultaneously, from the local to the national. Crossing institutional walls can be a great way to learn from the successes and failures of others who have more experience with digital projects than you, especially as you are starting out. It's worth at least exploring the potential benefits that collaboration can bring to your institution.

REFERENCES

Christenson, Heather. 2011. "HathiTrust: A Research Library at Web Scale." *Library Resources and Technical Services* 55, no. 2: 93–102. https://www.hathitrust.org/documents/christenson-lrts-201104.pdf.

Coyle, Karen. 2006. "Mass Digitization of Books." *Journal of Academic Librarianship* 32, no. 6: 641–45. doi: 10.1016/j.acalib.2006.08.002.

HathiTrust Digital Library. 2016. "Update on Spring Activities." https://www.hathitrust.org/2016-spring-update.

Kahle, Brewster. 2007. "Universal Access to All Knowledge." *American Archivist* 70, no. 1: 23–31.

Kelly, Kevin. 2006. "Scan This Book!" *New York Times Magazine*. May 14: 42–49, 65, 71. www.nytimes.com/2006/05/14/magazine/14publishing.html?_r=0.

Middleton, Ken, and Mayo Taylor. 2010. "Collaborative Digitization Goes Local." In *Digitization in the Real World: Lessons Learned from Small and Medium-Sized Digitization Projects,* edited by Kwong Bor Ng and Jason Kucsma, 435–49. New York: Metropolitan New York Library Council.

Neatrour, Anna, Rebekah Cummings, and Sandra McIntyre. 2016. "Regional Aggregation and Discovery of Digital Collections: The Mountain West Digital Library." In *Exploring Discovery: The Front Door to Your Library's Licensed and Digitized Content,* edited by Ken Varnum, 219–32. Chicago: American Library Association.

Raab, Christopher. 2007. "From the ACRL 13th National Conference: Collaborative Solutions to Digitization for College Library Special Collections." *College & Undergraduate Libraries* 14, no. 4: 37–48. doi: 10.1080/10691310802046777.

Wu, Tim. 2015. "What Ever Happened to Google Books?" *The New Yorker.* September 11. www.newyorker.com/business/currency/what-ever-happened-to-google-books.

PART II
BASIC SKILLS

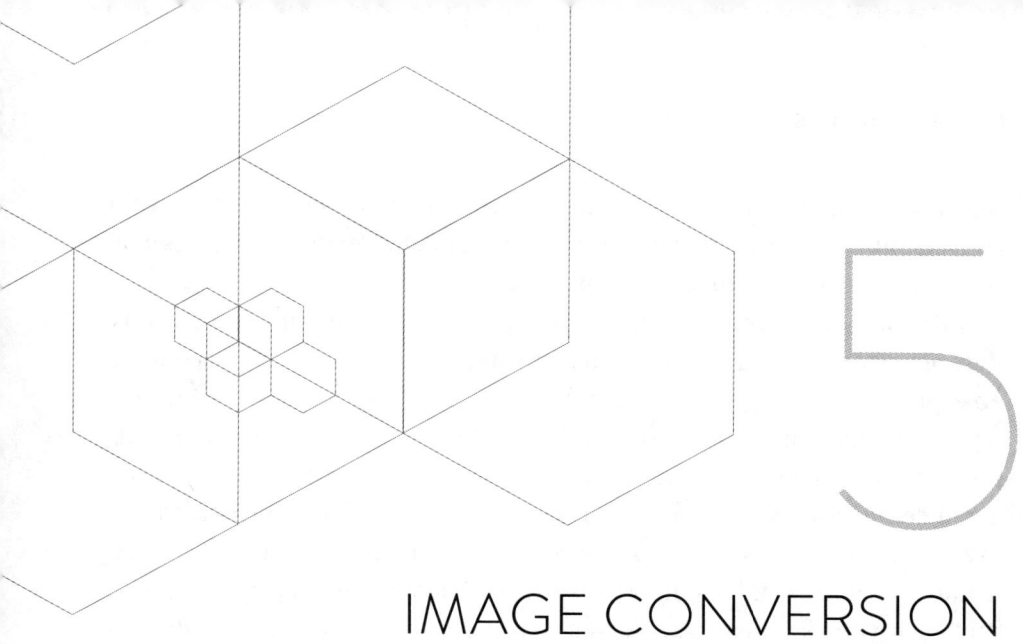

IMAGE CONVERSION

MONG ALL THE MAJOR STEPS INVOLVED IN BUILDING A digital collection—selecting content, reformatting objects from analog to digital format, creating metadata, and delivering the content online—the reformatting, or digital conversion, process may at first glance appear to be the simplest and most straightforward. After all, how difficult can it be to place a photo or document in a scanner, hit "scan," and save the resulting file to a computer? The physical steps involved are, admittedly, fairly effortless. However, there is a good amount of background knowledge required to create digital surrogates that are true to the original and capture all the detail contained within it. A digital collection is not very useful to its users if the image, audio, or video files it contains are of low quality, or do not reflect an accurate representation of the original source material. Certain standards exist in the cultural heritage community for the creation of archival-quality digital objects, and it's important to have an understanding of these best practices before you embark on any digitization project. While relatively simple, the process of digital conversion can be tedious and time-consuming, and it's imperative to ensure the job is done adequately the first time around so as to avoid having to repeat it. And in the case of old and fragile materials, in which the act of digital conversion can contribute to further damage or deterioration to the original, the process is best not undertaken more than once.

This chapter will cover the basics of digital images, and introduce you to best practices for image reformatting and conversion. You do not need to be an expert in this area, but it helps to have a working knowledge of various file types and their appropriate uses, as well as the different strategies and technologies available for converting your analog materials to digital form. Even if you do not reformat your materials yourself but have them outsourced to a third party for conversion, you still need to understand the topic well enough to know what to ask for and how to use the digital files once you receive them. And while you may create your digital collections entirely out of "born digital" materials, precluding the need for analog-to-digital conversion, these digital files may eventually need to be reformatted for preservation purposes (see chapter 9 for a more detailed discussion of this subject). We will focus in this chapter on pictorial and textual documents, since they tend to form the core of most digital collections. Learning the basics of digital image conversion will place you in a good position to progress to other forms of digital media, namely audio and video.

What Is a Digital Image?

The digital images we will be discussing in this chapter are a type of graphic known as a *raster* or *bitmap* image (as opposed to *vector* images, which are more closely associated with graphics created by drawing software or computer-aided design applications). Raster images result from the conversion of analog data into digital data by a measuring process known as sampling (Note 2011). Raster images are comprised of *pixels,* or "picture elements," tiny points that are arranged in a grid of rows and columns within the image. Each pixel contains one color, and it is the variations in color and brightness in individual pixels that creates the detail we see in a digital image. The colors in individual pixels are represented in binary code (strings of binary digits, or *bits,* that are made up of ones and zeros), and this code is stored in the file and interpreted by a computer for display on a screen.

RESOLUTION

The *spatial resolution* of a digital image refers to the level of spatial detail that it contains, with higher resolution denoting greater detail, clarity, and sharpness. Resolution is expressed in pixels per inch (ppi) or the often-interchangeably used dots per inch (dpi); it is essentially a measurement of the density of pixels in a given area and is dependent on pixel size. The ppi represents the sampling frequency, or the rate at which an image is sampled during scanning. If you compare a rate of 72 pixels per inch with 300 pixels per inch, the latter sampling frequency results in a smaller pixel size, more data captured from the original image, and thus greater detail. In other words, the more pixels per inch, the more accurately the digital representation can portray the original image (Boss 2001). Consequently, a higher resolution image will result in a larger file size because there is more information stored. You will not notice a difference in spatial resolution when you view an image on a screen, only when you print it—a lower resolution image will appear "pixelated" or blocky. The *pixel dimensions* of an image are its horizontal and vertical measurements expressed in pixels, and can be determined by multiplying the width and height in inches by the ppi.

COLOR AND TONE

In addition to spatial resolution, a digital image is also measured in terms of its levels of color or tonality. An image may be *bitonal, grayscale,* or *color.* Bitonal images contain strictly black or white values, while grayscale can contain the range of neutral shades between black and white. Color images can capture a much broader range of tonal value. The number of tones that can be represented by an image is related to its *bit depth* (also known as *color depth*), which can be thought of as the amount of storage space allocated to an individual pixel. Each individual pixel has a certain number of bits assigned to it, and the greater the number of bits per pixel, the greater the number of tones that can be represented.

A bitonal image has a bit depth of one, meaning it only has one bit available per pixel, which can contain one of two possible values (black or white). A grayscale image can store multiple values per bit, allowing for varying gradations of gray. As bit depth increases, the number of available tones increases exponentially, so a two-bit image can store four possible values (2^2), while an eight-bit image can store 256 (2^8). Grayscale images typically range in value from two to sixteen bits, with eight-bit being a common standard (in which case, a pixel has the capacity for one of 256 shades of gray). Color images generally have a bit depth of at least eight, with twenty-four being a general benchmark within the cultural heritage community. At 2^{24} available values, a 24-bit color image has 16.7 million different colors that can be assigned to a single pixel. While larger bit-depths are available, for example thirty-two and forty-eight, they result in extremely large file sizes and cannot be displayed on most computer monitors.

Color images are also associated with a concept known as *color space* (sometimes referred to as a *color profile*). A color space is a defined range of colors that is available to a particular device or file. Similar in a way to an artist's palette of paints, it is the set of colors (or "gamut") that, for example, a monitor is able to display or a printer is able to print. A color space is a particular instance of a *color model*. A computer monitor or digital camera uses the RGB (red-green-blue) color model, as opposed to the CMYK (cyan-magenta-yellow-black) color model that is used in offset printing. The RGB color model is most commonly used for capturing image files that will be viewed on a computer screen. Within the RGB color model there are a number of color spaces, such as sRGB and Adobe RGB. sRGB is most commonly used, and is considered the default color space of the Web and most computers.

A color model contains a certain number of *color channels* that store the color information for each of the primary color components. Whereas grayscale images use only one channel, color images use three channels, one each for red, green, and blue. A 24-bit RGB color image can be described as being eight bits per channel: three channels multiplied by eight bits per channel, for a total of twenty-four bits. Therefore, each pixel is encoded with a possible 256 shades of red, green, and blue. Since the amount of total bits per pixel is relative to the size of the file, a 24-bit color image will also be three times the size of an eight-bit color or grayscale image (Bogus et al. 2013).

COMPRESSION

When reformatting an image, the file size increases in relation to the surface area of the original document and the bit depth and spatial resolution at which it is scanned. High-resolution color images, in particular, can be quite large, causing issues for storage, processing, and transmission. Image files can be reduced in size by a process known as *compression*. Compression is achieved using an algorithm that reduces the amount of data required to represent a digital image, using the strategies of redundancy reduction and irrelevancy reduction. These compression techniques may be standard (open) or proprietary.

The strategy of redundancy reduction, in which data compression is achieved by coding redundant data in a more efficient manner, is known as *lossless* compression. With lossless compression techniques, no data is lost during the process and the decompressed file will be exactly the same as the original file, bit for bit. Irrelevancy reduction applies to the technique of *lossy* compression, in which smaller file size is achieved by discarding the least significant data in the image. While a loss of image quality does result, depending on the level of compression applied this data loss may not be detectable to the naked eye, making the image "visually lossless." Lossy compression may result in "artifacts" or defects in the image, which while initially imperceptible may accumulate if the file is edited and saved many times. Lossy compression produces a much higher reduction in file size than lossless compression, but does so with some degree of sacrifice to image quality and file integrity.

Image File Formats

As with compression techniques, there are both standard and proprietary image file formats. In the cultural heritage community, it is recommended that nonproprietary formats be used whenever possible. This allows for device independence and enduring viability: the files do not require a specific software or operating system, and they will not fall out of use if a company stops supporting them. Standard formats can also be shared and reused with greater ease, which is especially important when participating in cooperative projects. The following are common standard file formats for use with digital images.

TIFF (TAGGED IMAGE FILE FORMAT)

The name of this file format relates to the fact that TIFF files contain a set of tags for recording technical metadata such as image size and color space. The TIFF format does support both lossy and lossless compression, but the files are by default uncompressed, and are used for capturing high-quality bitonal, grayscale, and color images without any loss of information from the original. As a result of their ability to capture rich detail, TIFF files can be quite large. As lossless files, they can be repeatedly edited and saved without degradation to the image that would otherwise occur due to compression loss.

JPEG (Joint Photographic Experts Group)

JPEG, a lossy compression technique, is the most common compression method applied to grayscale and color images. JPEG compressed files are much smaller than TIFFs, can be viewed in any web browser, and are compatible with most software applications. When creating a JPEG file, the degree of compression can be adjusted, allowing the user to control the balance between image quality and file size. The JPEG format is best used for "continuous tone" images such as photographs, rather than bitonal images like line drawings or text.

JPEG 2000

In 2000 the Joint Photographic Experts Group developed a new standard to supersede and improve upon the JPEG compression method and file format. JPEG 2000 employs a more efficient wavelet-based compression technique that results in better image quality at smaller file sizes with fewer visible artifacts. It can produce a visually lossless image with a significantly reduced storage footprint than an uncompressed TIFF file. JPEG 2000 is a multi-resolution file format, so users can extract from a single compressed file different versions at multiple resolution levels. JPEG 2000 also provides built-in zooming and panning features, allowing images to be enlarged to show details.

GIF (Graphics Interchange Format)

The GIF format uses lossless compression and is compatible with bitonal, grayscale, and color images. However, it only allows for eight-bit grayscale or color. This results in files that are small and efficient, but only suitable for a limited range of image types. GIF can also be used to create simple animations. Due to the limited range of colors available it is not a good choice for color photographs, but it may be appropriate in some cases for grayscale photos.

PNG (Portable Network Graphics)

PNG is a lossless format that was created in the 1990s as an open source replacement for GIF, resulting from concerns about licensing fees associated with the proprietary LZW compression technique that GIF uses (the LZW patent has since expired, making GIF free to use). Though it has not replaced GIF, it has become widely adopted for delivering images on the Web. PNG is more versatile then GIF, allowing for a color bit depth of up to forty-eight, thus permitting lossless compression of full-color images.

PDF (Portable Document Format) **AND PDF/ARCHIVAL**
Though it was created by the commercial entity Adobe Systems, the PDF file format has become a de facto standard for delivering documents on the Web—in fact, it was recognized as a standard by the International Organization for Standardization (ISO) in 2008. While originally a proprietary format, it has since become an open specification, meaning that the features and functions for the file format are made publicly available for other software developers to use in designing their products (Fanning 2008). However, Adobe's free Acrobat software is most commonly used for creating and accessing PDF files. The format is device- and resolution- independent (PDF files themselves have no resolution, although a raster image embedded within a PDF will). PDFs are widely used for delivering multipage documents that provide full-text search capability. ISO has also developed a family of standards, PDF/Archival (or PDF/A), that has gained traction in the archival community. The format is intended to support long-term preservation by limiting certain functionalities of traditional PDF files such as encryption, multimedia, and embedded files, because these elements could hinder future rendering of the document as technologies change.

Best Practices for Digital Image Capture

As you can see, when creating digital image files there are multiple variables involved including resolution, bit depth, and file format. Deciding how best to balance these variables can be tricky, but luckily there are established standards and best practices in the cultural heritage community that you can refer to for guidance. Individual institutions will often document their own sets of specifications, and these may vary to some degree from one another but they tend to adhere to the same general guidelines. If you participate in a cooperative digitization project it is likely that the managing institution, such as a consortium or state library, will provide its preferred specifications for you to follow. If you are starting from scratch, the following section outlines commonly followed rules for capturing digital images.

MASTER AND DERIVATIVE FILES

Standard practice is to first create a rich *master* image file, an initial digital version of the analog object that is stored for purposes of long-term archiving and preservation. This archival master should be of the highest quality possible in order to capture the maximum amount of information from the original. It is customary for master files to be saved as uncompressed, lossless TIFFs. These files are generally quite large, and are therefore not appropriate for web delivery (additionally, many browsers do not read TIFF files without the help of a plug-in). Therefore, *derivative* images of various sizes and file formats (typically lossy compression formats) are subsequently created from the master file, and these are used for specific purposes including access copies for online viewing and thumbnails for image browsing within a DCMS.

The general principle for master and derivative files is "capture once, use many times." For master files, it is usually preferable to scan from the earliest available version of an analog object, because each subsequent generation loses detail. Therefore, creating a master image from a photographic negative or book will yield a higher-quality product than from a photographic print, microfilm, or photocopy. At the same time, keep in mind that a digital image can only have as much detail as the original. Capturing lower-quality originals at higher resolutions will not necessarily improve their image quality, but it will increase file size. Since master files will take up significant amounts of storage space, the quality at which you capture them will be dependent on your budget and the amount of storage you have available. In general, the quality of your digital masters should be as high as you can afford. For a small institution this may mean just meeting the minimum recommended standards, while a large institution may have the capacity to significantly exceed these guidelines.

The JPEG file format is the standard choice for creating derivatives of continuous-tone images (such as photographs) for sharing via the Web or e-mail; due to their smaller size these files require less storage and can be downloaded quickly. Though they are lossy, the image quality of JPEGs is considered acceptable for online viewing and any loss of information is generally not noticeable to the naked eye. GIF files may be used as derivatives of line art and graphic images such as logos, charts, maps, and illustrations that contain a narrow range of color and tone. PNG may be suitable for these simple object types too, but due to its relatively large file size it has not replaced JPEG as the derivative format of choice for more complex color and grayscale images. PDFs may also be used as access derivatives for textual documents. Many institutions rely almost exclusively on JPEG for access versions of all object types.

It was initially thought that JPEG 2000 would come to replace TIFF in the cultural heritage community as the file format of choice for archival master files, and perhaps replace JPEG for derivatives. But so far its uptake has been slow to moderate, being described as "warmly embraced by some and the subject of anxiety by others" (FADGI 2014). Large institutions with particularly sizable digital collections, such as the Library of Congress, have been adopters of the standard, but in general TIFF and JPEG remain the norm. This is likely related to the complexity of the standard and to the fact that support is still fairly low for display and manipulation of JPEG 2000 files in common browsers, tools, and applications. JPEG 2000 is, however, better suited for online delivery of large-format images such as maps, because its wavelet-based image compression allows for efficient transmission and zooming and panning of large image files. Similarly, the PNG format may be suitable for archival master files due to its ability to capture lossless images at a high bit depth, but in reality it has not become widely accepted in the cultural heritage community for this purpose.

IMAGE RESOLUTION AND COLOR

There is no single perfect resolution at which to scan all types of materials, and ppi alone cannot be used as a measure of image quality. Resolution should be adjusted based on the size, quality, condition, and uses of the digital object. The combination of ppi and size of the original object determines the resolution needed to accurately capture as much information about the original object as is available (Thiel 2008). As Peterson points out, the question should not be "How high should the resolution be?" but rather, "What level of resolution captures enough information from the original object to be considered high resolution in the anticipated reproduction uses?" (2005).

Common practice is to create master files at a resolution of no less than 300 ppi. This is generally sufficient for plain text documents, although textual documents that contain images may benefit from a slightly higher resolution.

Photographs and other pictorial documents are typically scanned at higher resolutions, depending on the size of the original. While many institutions specify fixed ppi ranges for specific materials types, such as 300–600 ppi for a photographic print, others will specify a minimum spatial resolution such as 3,000 ppi across the longest side of the original. In this case, the appropriate resolution is determined by dividing the desired number of pixels by the length in inches of the long side of the original (e.g., 3000 / 5 for a 4 × 5 inch print, resulting in a resolution of 600 ppi). This technique more accurately reflects the relationship between spatial resolution and object size, with smaller objects benefiting from a higher resolution.

The bit depth at which a digital image is created will also affect various other aspects of the file. Increasing the bit depth enables the capture of more detail and results in better quality, but will affect resolution requirements, file size, and compression. Reducing bit depth will result in smaller file sizes but somewhat poorer quality (Zhang and Gourley 2009). Most guidelines recommended a minimum of eight-bit grayscale and 24-bit color. Bitonal imaging may be acceptable for black-and-white textual documents that display good contrast between the printed text and the paper background, but grayscale is often preferred for all noncolor documents in order to capture the tonal range of the original. While capturing color information when it does not contribute any additional information to the surrogate only increases file size and is often unnecessary (Note 2011), at the same time, capturing black-and-white and grayscale images in color can reveal details about the original object that may be of interest to some users, such as discoloration of paper or prints due to age. These considerations will need to be weighed along with storage constraints when deciding whether to capture certain images in grayscale or color.

Table 5.1 summarizes some suggested master file specifications for various types of materials. These reflect the minimum resolution that is generally accepted, though guidelines vary by institution. When determining your own set of imaging guidelines, it is a good idea to compare published best practices from a number of institutions. Some recommended standards and guidelines to consult are listed in the references at the end of this chapter (Bogus et al. 2013, Library of Congress 2006, Thiel 2008). Many more can be found with a simple Internet search.

TABLE 5.1
Sample master image file specifications by document type

Document Type	Minimum Resolution	Minimum Bit Depth
Black-and-white printed text, sheet music, microfilm	300–600 ppi	1-bit bitonal or 8-bit grayscale
Textual documents with images	400–600 ppi	8-bit grayscale or 24-bit RGB color
Manuscripts, photographic prints, illustrations	400–800 ppi	8-bit grayscale or 24-bit RGB color
Photographic negatives and slides	800–1,200 ppi	8-bit grayscale or 24-bit RGB color
Oversized materials	300–600 ppi	8-bit grayscale or 24-bit RGB color

IMAGE PROCESSING

In order to be faithful to the original, the master image file should typically not undergo any type of image processing or correction subsequent to capture. The only action to be taken on a master file is to save it in different file formats and/or resolutions for derivative copies. For example, you may save a second copy of a master TIFF in JPEG format at a resolution of 150 ppi for use as an access file, and a third JPEG or GIF copy at a resolution of 96 ppi for use as a thumbnail. Some DCMSs automatically create derivatives from an uploaded master file, so this step may not need to be done by hand.

If you use an image editing program to adjust the resolution of a file by hand, it's important to understand how resolution changes in relation to image dimensions. In order to maintain the same resolution when resizing an image, the number of pixels needs to be adjusted accordingly. As image size in inches increases, resolution decreases if the number of pixels is not also increased. Conversely, as image size in inches decreases, resolution increases if the number of pixels is not also decreased. Stated another way, you can make an image smaller by increasing the resolution (thereby moving the pixels closer together), or make an image larger by decreasing the resolution (which spaces the pixels farther apart). Images can also be resized by *resampling*, which creates a new version of an image with a different width or height in pixels. This is done through the process of *interpolation,* whereby pixels are inserted into or deleted from an image so as to maintain image resolution.

You may wish to carry out some type of image processing on derivative files, for example sharpening, straightening, cropping, color correction, or removing blemishes. It is generally a good idea to refrain from this type of activity except when necessary, since it is time-consuming but also because it can detract from the authenticity of the image. Adobe Photoshop is the standard software for editing image files, but Adobe's scaled-down, cheaper versions, Photoshop Elements and Photoshop Lightroom, are adequate for most basic editing tasks. Open source image-editing software such as GIMP (www.gimp.org), IrfanView (www.irfanview.com), and Paint.NET (www.getpaint.net) are also good, and free, options.

FILE NAMING CONVENTIONS

A final aspect of digital file creation that is important, but easily overlooked, is formulating conventions for naming your files. Files should have names that are consistent and pattern-based in order to assist with sorting, organization, and version control. File names may be descriptive or "opaque" (nondescriptive). Opaque file names may simply be sequential numbers and have no relationship to the item itself. Descriptive file names contain words, abbreviations, or numbers that signify something meaningful about the original item, such as dates, accession numbers, collection titles, or page numbers. Opaque file names may be appropriate for large collections, but for smaller ones, descriptive naming conventions have the advantage of making files easier to identify and manage.

There are no formal standards to adhere to when creating descriptive file names, but certain best practices are commonly followed. These include the following general rules:

- Use only alphanumeric characters (letters and numbers), preferably all lowercase or "CamelCase" (using capitalized letters rather than spaces to denote word separation).
- Avoid using special characters such as . / > < + = ' ^ | \ { } [ ] # , ; ? ! $ * &.
- Dashes (—) or underscores (_) may be used in place of spaces.
- Depending on the number of files in a collection, use leading zeros as placeholders (for example, file01.tif or file001.tif rather than file1.tif).

- Choose a standard format for dates, such as yyyymmdd.
- Be as brief as possible and avoid lengthy file names.
- Include version indicators when necessary, for example v01, v02, or final.

An example of a descriptive file name might be SC115_18610801_02.tif, denoting the second page of a letter dated August 1, 1861 that is part of special collection 115. Another possibility would be VavraDiary1963_012_v2.jpg for the second version of the twelfth page in a diary dated 1963 from the Robert Vavra collection. Different collections may require different types of naming structures. Whatever conventions you establish for naming your files, retain documentation of these guidelines as a reference for future collection managers.

Hardware for Digital Image Capture

When embarking upon a digitization program at your institution, you will likely need to purchase new equipment for digital image capture. While you may already have basic technology in use for everyday document scanning, it's a good idea to also invest in hardware that will capture the highest-quality images possible, will hold up well to repeated use, and can be devoted solely to digitization projects. At least one dedicated workstation set up in a relatively clean, dust-free location is recommended.

If you are digitizing mainly photographs and manuscripts, a high-resolution flatbed scanner may be sufficient to meet your needs. A good, professional-grade color scanner from a manufacturer like Canon, Epson, or Fujitsu can cost several hundred dollars, but these higher-end models will capture precise color and detail and ideally hold up under years of heavy use. A cheaper, entry-level scanner may meet minimum quality requirements but process images more slowly and need to be replaced in a much shorter time frame. When shopping for a scanner, look for a unit that will scan at a spatial resolution equal to or exceeding the benchmarks you have set for various material types. Scanning technology has advanced to the point that even low-end scanners can capture images at fairly high resolutions; however, you will want to be sure that you are selecting a scanner based on its optical resolution—the actual resolution that the scanner can capture—rather than its interpolated resolution—the resolution that it can achieve by adding pixels. If you are scanning large numbers of documents that are not rare or fragile, an automatic sheet feeder is a feature that can speed up scanning time considerably.

If you have large materials such as maps or newspapers that are too big for a standard-size flatbed scanner, you may consider investing in a large-format scanner. These can run in the thousands of dollars, so unless you have a large number of these materials to scan, it may be more cost-effective to outsource oversized items for conversion. The topic of outsourcing your digitization projects is discussed further at the end of this chapter.

Another option for oversized materials is an overhead or planetary scanner. These types of scanners consist of cameras or sensors mounted above the scanning bed. There is no lid and the scanning apparatus does not come into direct contact with the materials, so overhead scanners are a good choice for fragile materials of all sizes that may incur damage from being pressed flat on a flatbed scanner. Some overhead scanners come equipped with v-shaped cradles for books, which can help protect the spine from damage by holding the book open at an angle, as well as eliminating text distortions due to page curvature. Automatic page turning is another feature of some overhead scanners that can allow for fast, efficient high-volume scanning. Overhead scanners are generally the most costly option for image conversion, with higher-end models running in the tens of thousands of dollars. An overhead scanner with a book cradle may be a sound investment if you are digitizing rare and fragile books that you do not wish to outsource.

A more cost-effective alternative for capturing oversized materials, fragile books, and 3-D objects may be to use a simple 35-mm digital single lens reflex (DSLR) camera. These cameras can capture high-quality images at high speeds and provide flexibility for a number of shooting situations. Look for a camera with a minimum of ten megapixels. With the aid of a camera or copy stand, a book cradle, and appropriate lighting, it's possible to fashion your own do-it-yourself version of an overhead scanner for a fraction of the cost. Indeed, some commercial overhead scanners are made up of these separate components packaged together with a pair of DSLR cameras and specialized file management software.

If you have large numbers of photographic slides or negatives to digitize, a film scanner may also be worth investigating. These machines scan at higher resolutions, some up to 10,000 ppi. Different models can accommodate various formats of film and slides, with lower-end models typically limited to 35 mm and 110 film while pricier versions can handle larger formats like 4 × 5 inch or 120 film. For large volumes of slides or film, there are models that utilize slide magazines for batch scanning. Some flatbed scanners are also sold with film transparency units that can be mounted on the scanning bed, and these can be a good option if you do not have enough slides or negatives to warrant a dedicated film scanner. Many film scanners also come equipped with dust and scratch reduction technology such as Magic Touch or Digital ICE, which can remove surface defects and create cleaner-looking scans (although this does not negate the need to clean objects for scanning, as well as scanners themselves, with a cloth or compressed air to remove dust buildup).

Finally, you may wish to digitize your microfilm or microfiche collections. Microforms are extremely stable and enduring, lasting for hundreds of years in proper conditions, and therefore remain a highly valued format for long-term preservation. Many institutions maintain the use of microform for master preservation copies, and employ digital reformatting for the creation of access versions. If you have a large volume of microforms that you wish to digitize, a microfilm or microfiche scanner may be an appropriate purchase. However, these machines can be fairly expensive, so many organizations find it more economical to have this type of digitization outsourced.

In addition to the scanning equipment itself, thought must also be given to the computer hardware that accompanies it. When scanning digital images in particular, you will benefit from purchasing a dedicated computer that has as much speed and storage as your budget allows. You should generally follow these principles when selecting a digitization computer:

- Purchase as much RAM (random access memory) as possible to ensure faster processing speeds;
- Look for a computer with processors optimized for image conversion; and
- Purchase as much hard drive space as possible (Thiel 2008).

It's also important to have a monitor that can accurately display your scanned images. Technology has advanced to the point that even low-end LCD monitors now boast fairly high display resolutions, commonly around 1080 × 1224 ppi for a seventeen-inch screen, and this may be adequate for most digitization needs. If you anticipate doing heavy image editing or working with very high resolution images, it may be worth investing in a model with a higher resolution and larger screen.

Optical Character Recognition

If you are digitizing relatively modern text documents such as books, magazines, and newspapers, you will likely want to take advantage of optical character recognition (OCR) technology to make the images full-text searchable. OCR engines convert images of words and letters into machine-readable text files that can be indexed for searching. Many higher-end scanners come packaged with OCR software, and it is also possible to purchase or license these programs separately. Examples of commercial OCR software include ABBYY Finereader, OmniPage, PrimeOCR, and Adobe Acrobat. A notable open source OCR engine is Tesseract, which was originally developed by HP and has since come under development by Google. While highly regarded in terms of character accuracy, Tesseract itself does not have a user-friendly interface and is run as a command-line program. Free software such as OCRFeeder is available that provides a full user interface overlaying the Tesseract engine.

OCR software can be incredibly useful, but is not without its limitations. It generally does not work well with handwritten manuscripts, which will usually require a hand-typed transcript. Most OCR programs can convert some number of foreign languages, but these capabilities vary widely depending on the software. And while good OCR software can boast search and character accuracy of up to 99 percent, no program will achieve perfection. This is particularly true if you are running OCR on scans of poor quality or documents that contain unusual fonts or symbols, non-Latin characters, or complicated layouts. For mistake-free OCR, some level of manual correction is usually necessary. According to Cohen and Rosenzweig, studies have concluded that the time spent correcting a small number of OCR errors can exceed the cost of typing the document from scratch (2005). This is why many institutions will simply use the unedited "raw" OCR and accept a certain number of errors in the text. Depending on the size and nature of your project, the quality of your OCR software, and the importance of complete accuracy, you will need to weigh the pros and cons of spending time on manual OCR correction.

Outsourcing Digitization Activities

As mentioned previously, there are situations that may warrant outsourcing digital image conversion and other activities to a third-party vendor. These include small or one-off projects that require equipment your institution doesn't own and doesn't wish to purchase, and very large projects that can be completed more quickly and economically by a vendor. There are many advantages to this approach, and it often makes sense to leverage the expertise of an outside professional. Not only does the vendor take responsibility for the costs of technology and infrastructure, but project expenses and time frames can be clearly set. One disadvantage of doing in-house digitization, especially for institutions that are just starting out, is that it can be very difficult to accurately predict the cost per object in terms of staff hours and other expenses. Even institutions that have years of experience with in-house digitization will frequently outsource projects, in part because they have learned to recognize the point at which in-house digitization ceases to be cost-effective.

As outsourcing has become common, more and more companies have sprung up to offer a variety of digitization services, not limited solely to format conversion. These may include materials preparation (for example, disbanding and cleaning), metadata creation, and OCR processing. As with any area of business, some professionals will provide a better service than others, so it pays to be diligent in evaluating potential digitization vendors. Particularly for larger projects, you should seek and compare multiple vendor proposals, asking questions such as the following:

- What equipment and software does the vendor use, and what is their general workflow?
- Do they have experience working with cultural heritage materials or rare and fragile documents?
- Can they supply samples of their work and references from past clients, preferably other libraries, archives, or museums?
- Do they display an understanding of relevant standards and best practices?
- What are their quality control practices?
- What are their transport, handling, security, and storage procedures for both physical originals and digital surrogates?

- Do the proposed cost and time frame seem reasonable compared with other estimates you receive? Those that are extremely low or high may signal a red flag.

When negotiating a contract with a vendor, be sure you are clear about such issues as your expectations regarding technical specifications and acceptable quality of deliverables, ownership of project outputs (vendor should agree to relinquish all rights), and how error correction will be handled. During the project, you will need to be an active participant by ensuring you meet all agreed-upon deadlines for tasks such as delivery of materials and quality control checks. It is recommended that you verify samples of the vendor's work at multiple points during the project so that errors may be promptly addressed. Open communication with the vendor at all stages of a project is crucial for success.

For all the beneficial aspects of outsourcing, there are just as many valid reasons for completing a project in-house. Outsourcing requires surrendering a certain amount of local control, and it may not be practical or desirable to transport certain materials off-site. Those just starting out with digital projects may prefer to do the work themselves in order to build expertise and skills; it can be difficult to establish expectations and benchmarks for vendors if you have not gone through the steps of completing a digitization project yourself. Whether it makes sense to outsource or digitize in-house will depend largely on the nature and scale of each unique project, and many institutions utilize both approaches as needed. It's also worth noting that outsourcing need not be an either/or proposition. It's perfectly acceptable to take a hybrid approach to individual projects, utilizing professional services for some aspects like format conversion while completing other project phases, such as metadata creation, locally.

Final Thoughts

Digital media is a topic that can be expanded upon at much greater lengths than are possible to delve into for the purposes of this book, but the information outlined above provides the basic knowledge you need to start reformatting and working with digital images. You may have other types of analog materials that you would like to digitize as well, such as cassette tapes, vinyl records, reel-to-reel film, and videotapes. Some of the general concepts discussed here will also be applicable to digital audio and video, including file compression, file naming conventions, and outsourcing. Other details, such as file formats, measures of quality, standard digitization guidelines, and types of reformatting equipment will differ and require further reading.

Once you have local guidelines determined and workflows in place, the process of digital conversion can usually be completed by anyone who has undergone some basic training in the relevant equipment and software, whether that be a paraprofessional, student worker, or volunteer. While delegating digitization tasks is the most efficient way to get projects completed quickly, it also necessitates vigilance on the part of collection managers to ensure that output is consistent. Some level of quality control should be built into the workflow; depending on the size and nature of the project, this may mean reviewing every file or doing random checks of a certain percentage of the whole. Once you have struck a successful balance between speed and quality in your production workflow, you will be able to take a step back and focus on other aspects of your project such as metadata, which is the focus of the next chapter.

REFERENCES

Bogus, Ian, George Blood, Robin L. Dale, Robin Leech, and David Mathews. 2013. "Minimum Digitization Capture Recommendations." Association for Library Collections and Technical Services Preservation and Reformatting Section. www.ala.org/alcts/resources/preserv/minimum-digitization-capture-recommendations.

Boss, Richard W. 2001. *Imaging for Libraries and Information Centers.* Library Technology Reports, vol. 37, no. 1 (January-February).

Cohen, Daniel J., and Roy Rosenzweig. 2005. "Digital History: A Guide to Gathering, Preserving, and Presenting the Past on the Web." http://chnm.gmu.edu/digitalhistory.

Fanning, Betsy A. 2008. *Preserving the Data Explosion: Using PDF.* DPC Technology Watch Series Report 08-02. www.dpconline.org/component/docman/doc_download/86-preserving-the-data-explosion-using-pdf-preserving-the-data-explosion-using-pdf.

Federal Agencies Digitization Guidelines Initiative (FADGI) Working Group. 2014. "Raster Still Images for Digitization: A Comparison of File Formats." www.digitizationguidelines.gov/guidelines/raster_stillImage_compare.html.

Library of Congress. 2006. "Technical Standards for Digital Conversion of Text and Graphic Materials." https://memory.loc.gov/ammem/about/techStandards.pdf.

Note, Margot. 2011. *Managing Image Collections: A Practical Guide*. Oxford: Chandos.

Peterson, Kit A. 2005. "Introduction to Basic Measures of a Digital Image for Pictorial Collections." Library of Congress Prints and Photographs Division. https://www.loc.gov/rr/print/tp/IntroDgtlImage.pdf.

Thiel, Sarah Goodwin, ed. 2008. "BCR's CDP Digital Imaging Best Practices, Version 2.0." Digital Imaging Best Practices Working Group. http://hdl.handle.net/1808/11174.

Zhang, Allison B., and Don Gourley. 2009. *Creating Digital Images: A Practical Guide*. Oxford: Chandos.

6

METADATA

ALONG WITH HIGH-QUALITY DIGITAL OBJECTS AND A FUNCtional DCMS, good metadata is perhaps the most important aspect of a user-friendly digital collection. Before we go into why this is, or even what metadata itself is, consider this thought experiment. Imagine that you have a number of digital photographs taken with one or more cameras, which you have uploaded to your computer. Imagine also that you have managed to erase all of the identifying information that accompanies each photograph—the file name, the date it was taken, the file size, the exposure time, the make and model of camera that it was taken with, and so on. There is simply a group of images that is sitting on your computer desktop, devoid of any type of description. How would you use this collection? How would you look through the files to find a specific photograph that was taken on a particular date with a particular camera, or find all of the photographs that were taken on a particular date in a particular location? In this case, you would be required to examine every single photograph individually and guess from its appearance whether or not it met the criteria you are looking for. For anything but the smallest collection, this would be an entirely inefficient and frustrating approach to accessing and using the digital objects contained within it. In fact, it would render the collection all but unusable.

This exercise exemplifies the importance of metadata for digital collections. Without it, digital objects would lack meaning and context for virtually all users. Furthermore, the collections themselves would be more or less invisible. Imagine that you have rebooted the computer in our thought experiment. Without file names, titles, or other identifying information to search for, how would you even locate the photographs to begin with? They would, for all intents and purposes of the user, not exist.

What Is Metadata?

While the above example is admittedly an extreme one, it does help to illustrate why good metadata is crucial for users of digital collections. But what exactly is metadata? The standard definition is "data about data," or "information about information," a very broad definition that has been parsed in great detail by various writers. Paul Miller describes metadata as "extra baggage" associated with a resource, "a means by which largely meaningless data may be transformed into information, interpretable and reusable by those other than the creator of the data resource" (Miller 2004). In essence, metadata is structured data that is associated with an information resource. It may be either created by hand or captured by a computer system. For example, when you create a Microsoft Word document, the system automatically generates certain information about the document, including the file size and the date the document was created or modified. However, you may also create your own values for properties such as title and file name. In digital collections, there is generally a combination of system and user-generated metadata used. Metadata may be embedded directly within the resource it is about, as Microsoft Word properties are embedded in the file, or it may be stored in a database that is separate from the resource.

Metadata can be associated with virtually any type of information resource, from analog to digital. Metadata is often thought of as belonging primarily to the digital realm, as it is used to describe image, audio, and video files as well as things like websites and data sets. But the Machine-Readable Cataloging (MARC) bibliographic records in a library catalog also constitute metadata about the items in the collection, functioning as stand-ins for physical objects such as books, serials, and videos. In all its forms, metadata essentially acts as a surrogate for the object it describes, and allows users to interact with the resource and perform certain functions (searching, browsing, etc.) without having to inspect the physical item.

Metadata is everywhere, and is not strictly associated with what we typically think of as information resources. The nutrition facts on a package of food can be considered a form of metadata about the package's contents, and the credits of a movie qualify as metadata about the film. Metadata is found in many contexts and utilized in some form in many professional communities, from education and publishing to health care and science. In the cultural heritage sector, there are a number of metadata standards that are commonly used, the most ubiquitous being Dublin Core. These standards will be discussed in more depth later in the chapter.

It is often more useful to talk about metadata in terms of what it does rather than what it is. At its most basic, metadata "enables people to perform certain functions in relation to the information resources that the metadata is about" (Miller 2011). Metadata can be described in terms of its functionality, which includes finding, identifying, sorting, selecting, gathering, obtaining, and navigating items within collections of resources. Because it is structured according to certain sets of rules, metadata can be interpreted and displayed by computer software and thus enables users to discover and retrieve resources via library catalogs and other systems. The purpose of metadata can be articulated in terms of supporting certain user tasks such as search and discovery, browsing and collocation, identification, and access (Phillips 2013).

Types of Metadata

Because metadata serves various purposes, it is often categorized into three overarching types according to the functionality it performs.

Descriptive metadata: descriptive metadata, as its name implies, is data that describes an object. Metadata that would fall under the heading of descriptive includes creator or author, title, date of creation, type of object, and subject or keyword associated with the object. Descriptive metadata is closely associated with the functionalities of searching and browsing, and is what makes it possible for you to discover and identify objects within a collection. Descriptive metadata is generally the most important type for users because it provides intellectual access to a collection's resources. It is the type of data they view directly when interacting with the front end of a digital collection.

Administrative metadata: administrative metadata is data that contributes to the management and administration of objects within a collection. This includes data such as date of digitization, type of equipment used for digitization, file name, and name of the organization that created the digital object. Administrative metadata comprises both technical and preservation metadata, and is generally used for internal management of digital resources (Puglia, Reed, and Rhodes 2004). Administrative metadata may also include information about the rights associated with an object, for example a copyright statement or restrictions on use and reproduction of the object. This type of metadata provides information that allows those in charge of a collection to manage the resources within it.

Structural metadata: many digital collections are comprised of compound objects, an example being a book or other textual resource that is made up of individual page images that may be organized into chapters and other sections such as tables of contents or indexes. Structural metadata indicates how these separate pieces are related to each other, how they are logically grouped and presented on the screen. It provides information about the internal or "physical" structure of a digital resource, ties component parts together to form a coherent whole, and provides navigational structure to complex objects. In describing an object's individual components and their relationships, structural metadata allows for the presentation of characteristics such as pagination, sequence, and synchronization between related objects.

When working with metadata, it is wise to keep in mind that these categories are fluid. Depending on the situation, a piece of metadata may fit the criteria for one or more types, serving multiple functions at the same time.

Metadata Terminology

The world of metadata has an associated vocabulary that may be rather bewildering to those who are unfamiliar with it. The following mini-glossary will therefore facilitate further discussion by demystifying some of these terms.

- *Element*—a property or attribute of the resource, for example *Title, Date,* or *File Size.* Elements serve as "containers" for data and can also be thought of as the equivalent of fields in a database.
- *Value*—the content (terms or words) that is used to populate an element or field, for example the value *Hamlet* applied to the element *Title.* The pairing of a data element with a data value constitutes a basic unit of metadata.
- *Record*—a collection or grouping of element-value pairs, functioning as a surrogate for a given resource.
- *Standard*—a set of guidelines or specifications for metadata structure or content. A metadata standard may be a scheme that has been developed and maintained by a standard organization or other group.
- *Scheme*—a structured collection or set of elements designed for a specific purpose, such as describing a particular type of information source; an implementation of a metadata standard (also known as an *element set*).
- *Application profile*—a set of domain-specific rules documenting a metadata scheme for a particular purpose, spelling out the element set and associated content guidelines (also known as a *data dictionary* or *best practice guide*).
- *Extensible Markup Language (XML)*—a markup language that is similar to HTML and can be used to encode metadata for machine processing and exchange.
- *Granularity*—the level of detail with which a resource or collection is described. The greater the granularity, the deeper the level of detail.

Metadata Standards

In order to start working effectively with metadata, you need to be familiar with the concept of standards and understand how to adapt them for use with your local digital collections. Standards are important because they provide for consistency in the creation of metadata values, which is crucial for functionalities such as searching, browsing, and sharing metadata between collections and repositories. Standards also provide structure to the way metadata is expressed in such a way that allows it to be machine-readable. Standards in various forms are common in other contexts in the cultural heritage community. Some examples you may be familiar with that relate to the description of physical materials include the Anglo-American Cataloging Rules (AACR), Describing Archives: A Content Standard (DACS), the Library of Congress Subject Headings (LCSH), and Cataloging Cultural Objects (CCO).

It may be useful to think of standards as being grouped into types depending on the purposes they serve. Gilliland defines four commonly accepted categories: data *structure* standards, data *value* standards, data *content* standards, and data *format/technical interchange* standards (Gilliland 2008). Data structure standards are sets of metadata elements or fields, and are commonly referred to as *schemes* (or often *schemas*) or *element sets;* the MARC format is an example of a structure standard. Data value standards are lists of established terms, codes, or names that are used in creating values that are entered into element fields; examples include controlled vocabularies such as LCSH and thesauri like the Art & Architecture Thesaurus (AAT). Data content standards constitute rules or best practices that dictate the correct format for creating non-standardized values that are entered into element fields; AACR, DACS, and CCO are examples of these. Data format/technical interchange standards provide specifications for encoding metadata in such a way that it may be processed by computers and exchanged between systems; XML is the most common example of this type. There is often overlap between data format standards and data structure standards in that many format standards may be encoded or marked up using XML.

For the purposes of this book we will focus on standards that are widely used, formally established, and maintained by a national or international agency or organization, although it is also possible to create your own local, informal sets of guidelines for a single digital repository or institution. There are many formally established metadata standards that have been developed for various purposes and user communities; Jenn Riley maps out 105 of them in her chart "Seeing Standards: A Visualization of the Metadata Universe" (Riley 2009). While this number may seem overwhelming, a small subset of these standards is most widely used for digital collections in the cultural heritage sector. Four of the most commonly found structure standards for digital content are summarized below.

DUBLIN CORE ELEMENT SET (DCMES)

The Dublin Core Element Set (DCMES) is so called because it originated at a 1995 workshop hosted by the Online Computer Library Center (OCLC) at its headquarters in Dublin, Ohio. A governing body, the Dublin Core Metadata Initiative (DCMI), was developed to manage and oversee Dublin Core and its related specifications. The DCMES has been adopted as a formal standard by the International Organization for Standardization (ISO) and the National Information Standards Organization (NISO).

Dublin Core is perhaps the most commonly found data structure standard in the cultural heritage sector because it was developed to be simple, broad, and generic enough for use in a "cross-disciplinary information environment" (NISO 2013). For this reason, it is a good starting point for those new to metadata. Dublin Core was originally created to describe web-based resources, but it may be used with other types of materials as well. It is comprised of fifteen core elements that are known as "simple" Dublin Core. Eventually, a set of *qualifiers* was developed that could be used as subproperties of some original elements to extend them and give them a greater degree of granularity. There are two categories of qualifiers, those that further refine an element meaning (known as *refinements*) and those that identify controlled vocabularies or other encoding schemes that could be used in representing an element's value.

Originally, when a refinement was added to a simple Dublin Core element, it was expressed in the format *Element.Refinement* (for example, "Title.Alternative"). In recent years, the DCMI has updated its recommendations so that the word "qualifier" has been superseded by "refinement," and refinements may now be expressed as stand-alone terms apart from the core elements they refine (for example, simply *Alternative* for a secondary title). As Zeng and Qin point out, both usages may co-exist in practice (Zeng and Qin 2016). Table 6.1 defines the fifteen core elements, their definitions, and the optional refinements that correspond with certain ones in order to narrow their meaning or scope (those identifying controlled vocabularies or encoding schemes are not included). Further documentation and information about Dublin Core can be found at the DCMI website, www.dublincore.org.

TABLE 6.1
Simple Dublin Core element set with refinements

Element	Definition	Refinements	
Title	A name given to the resource	Alternative	
Creator	An entity primarily responsible for making the resource		
Contributor	An entity responsible for making contributions to the resource		
Description	An account of the resource	Table of Contents	Abstract
Publisher	An entity responsible for making the resource available		
Date	A point or period of time associated with an event in the life cycle of the resource	Created Valid Available Issued	Modified Date Accepted Date Copyrighted Date Submitted
Subject	The topic of the resource		
Language	A language of the resource		
Type	The nature or genre of the resource		
Format	The file format, physical medium, or dimensions of the resource	Extent	Medium
Coverage	The spatial or temporal topic of the resource, the spatial applicability of the resource, or the jurisdiction under which the resource is relevant	Spatial	Temporal
Source	A related resource from which the described resource is derived		

Element	Definition	Refinements	
Identifier	An unambiguous reference to the resource within a given context	Bibliographic Citation	
Relation	A related resource	Is Version Of Has Version Is Replaced By Replaces Is Required By Requires Is Part Of	Has Part Is Referenced By References Is Format Of Has Format Conforms To
Rights	Information about rights held in and over the resource	Access Rights License	

METADATA OBJECT DESCRIPTION SCHEMA (MODS)

Metadata Object Description Schema commonly goes by the acronym MODS. This structure standard is derived from the MARC 21 Format for Bibliographic Data, the encoding standard used for library catalog data. For this reason, it is widely used in the library community but is also general enough to be applied to a wide range of resources in the cultural heritage sector. MODS can be used to encode data from existing MARC records, or it can be used to create original metadata records from scratch. The MODS standard was developed by the Library of Congress and is maintained by that organization's Network Development and MARC Standards Office; detailed documentation about the scheme can be found at the website www.loc.gov/standards/mods.

MODS is frequently expressed using the XML markup language, which uses tags to demarcate elements. When encoded this way, it is known as MODS-XML. An understanding of XML is useful for working with MODS and other XML-based metadata standards, but it is not necessarily a requirement for those creating metadata using these standards. A detailed discussion of XML is beyond the scope of this book, but for those who wish to learn more, a good place to start is the w3schools.com XML tutorial at www.w3schools.com/xml/default.asp.

MODS has come to be a popular element set because it provides for richer resource description (greater granularity) than Dublin Core, and its basis in

MARC 21 makes it highly compatible with library data. MODS is more complex than Dublin Core in that it uses a set of nested, hierarchical elements and sub-elements. The twenty top-level elements and their definitions are presented in table 6.2. Similar to Dublin Core refinements, MODS also makes use of *attributes* that can further refine the meaning or scope of an element or identify an authority or encoding schema to use for an element value. MODS subelements and attributes and their definitions can be found in the *Detailed Description of MODS Elements* at www.loc.gov/standards/mods/v3/mods-userguide-elements.html#titleinfo.

TABLE 6.2
MODS top-level elements

Element Name	Definition
titleInfo	A word, phrase, character, or group of characters, normally appearing in a resource, that names it or the work contained in it
name	The name of a person, organization, or event (conference, meeting, etc.) associated in some way with the resource
typeOfResource	A term that specifies the characteristics and general type of content of the resource
genre	A term(s) that designates a category characterizing a particular style, form, or content, such as artistic, musical, literary composition, etc.
originInfo	Information about the origin of the resource, including place of origin or publication, publisher/originator, and dates associated with the resource
language	A designation of the language in which the content of a resource is expressed
physicalDescription	Describes the physical attributes of the information resource
abstract	A summary of the content of the resource
tableOfContents	A description of the contents of a resource
targetAudience	A description of the intellectual level of the audience for which the resource is intended
note	General textual information relating to a resource

Element Name	Definition
subject	A term or phrase representing the primary topic(s) on which a work is focused
classification	A designation applied to a resource that indicates the subject by applying a formal system of coding and organizing resources according to subject area
relatedItem	Information that identifies other resources related to the one being described
identifier	A unique standard or code that distinctively identifies a resource
location	Identifies the institution or repository holding the resource, or an electronic location in the form of a URL where it is available
accessCondition	Information about restrictions imposed on access to a resource
part	The designation of physical parts of a resource in a detailed form
extension	Provides additional information not covered by MODS
recordInfo	Information about the metadata record

VISUAL RESOURCE ASSOCIATION CORE CATEGORIES

The Visual Resources Association (VRA) Core Categories metadata scheme is a descriptive structure standard that was originally developed by the VRA and is now jointly hosted by the Library of Congress and the VRA. VRA Core is intended to be used to describe works of visual culture (for example, art and architecture) and is therefore utilized primarily by museums, although it may be used in other areas of the cultural heritage community as well. The VRA Core element set was originally based on the Dublin Core model, and has since evolved into a more MODS-like XML-based schema. The current version of the standard, VRA Core 4, contains nineteen elements (listed in table 6.3) as well as a number of associated sub-elements and attributes.

VRA Core is uniquely suited for use in the museum community in that it differentiates between the concepts of *work, image,* and *collection,* and requires that each of these object types have their own separate records to be linked together in a local database via the *relation* element. A *work* is defined as a built or created object, such as a piece of art that a museum owns, while an *image* is a visual representation of that object, for example a slide or photograph. A *collection* is an aggregate of these objects, and this type of record allows for collection-level cataloging of groups of works or images.

VRA Core 4 is also distinctive in that it exists in two different versions. The unrestricted version allows for any value to be entered into any of the elements, sub-elements, or attributes, while the restricted version imposes requirements on the values that may be entered into the *type* attributes that accompany various elements. Documentation about the two versions of the standard, along with other detailed information, can be found at the VRA Core website, www.loc.gov/standards/vracore/.

TABLE 6.3
VRA Core 4 elements

Element	Definition
Work, Collection, or Image	A choice of one of these three elements defines a record as describing a WORK (a built or created object), a COLLECTION (an aggregate of such objects), or an IMAGE (a visual surrogate of such objects)
Agent	Names or other identifiers assigned to an individual, group, or corporate body that has contributed to the design, creation, production, manufacture, or alteration of the object
Cultural Context	Name of the culture or people from which a work, collection, or image originates, or the cultural context with which it has been associated
Date	Date or range of dates associated with the creation, design, production, presentation, performance, construction, alteration, etc. of the object
Description	Note, including comments, description, or interpretation, that gives additional information not recorded in other categories
Inscription	Marks or written words added to the object at the time of production or in its subsequent history, including signatures, dates, dedications, texts, and colophons, and stamps
Location	Geographic location and/or name of the repository, building, site, or other entity whose boundaries include the work or image
Material	Substance of which a work or an image is composed
Measurements	Physical size, shape, scale, dimensions, or format of the object

Element	Definition
Relation	Terms or phrases describing the identity of the related work and the relationship between the work being cataloged and the related object
Rights	Information about the copyright status and the rights holder
Source	Reference to the source of the information recorded about the object
State Edition	Identifying number and/or name assigned to the state or edition of a work that exists in more than one form and the placement of that work in the context of prior or later issuances of multiples of the same work
Style Period	Defined style, historical period, group, school, dynasty, movement, etc. whose characteristics are represented in the work or image
Subject	Terms or phrases that describe, identify, or interpret the work or image and what it depicts or expresses
Technique	Production or manufacturing processes, techniques, and methods incorporated in the fabrication or alteration of the work or image
Textref	Name of a related textual reference and any type of unique identifier that text assigns to a work or collection that is independent of any repository
Title	Title or identifying phrase given to a work or an image
Work Type	Specific type of work, collection, or image being described in the record

ENCODED ARCHIVAL DESCRIPTION (EAD)

Encoded Archival Description, or EAD, originated in the archival community in 1998 and is most heavily used in academic libraries, historical societies, and museums with large special collections. This structure standard is maintained jointly by the Library of Congress and the Society for American Archivists; the official website containing further background and schema documentation is at www.loc.gov/ead/.

EAD differs from standards such as Dublin Core, MODS, and VRA Core in that it was developed primarily for collection-level rather than item-level description. The standard was created specifically to encode archival finding aids; these are textual documents that serve as inventories or indexes and provide information about the content and intellectual organization of archival and manuscript collections. The result is that EAD-encoded finding aids may be searched, browsed, and displayed in an online environment, and they allow for the standardization of collection information in finding aids within and across repositories. EAD finding aids may also provide access to digital images and item transcriptions via linking, but the general scope of the standard is not to provide description of individual items in a collection.

EAD expressed using XML markup is known as EAD-XML. The second version of the standard, EAD 2002, contains nearly 150 elements and dozens of attributes, making it much more complex than the three previously discussed standards. However, only nine elements are required for an EAD document to be considered "valid," so the complexity of description used is highly dependent on the needs of the individual collection. This flexibility can make information exchange between different institutions somewhat difficult. In partial response to this challenge, a revised version of the standard, EAD3, was released in 2015 and has replaced EAD 2002 as the official version. The aims of this major revision included improving EAD exchange between institutions, improving interoperability between EAD and other archival standards, and shifting the emphasis toward data encoding over data presentation and display. EAD3 introduces 52 new elements, some of which replace or refine elements in EAD 2002, and removes 33 existing elements.

Creating a Metadata Scheme

Now that you have a basic familiarity with metadata standards—what they are, and which ones are frequently used in the cultural heritage community—you are ready to explore the process of designing a metadata scheme for a particular set of digital resources. Your scheme may be for an individual digital collection or a group of collections. In designing your scheme, you may elect to follow an established standard very closely—for example, you may decide to use some or all of the fifteen Dublin Core elements and stop there. Or you may select various elements from multiple existing metadata standards and combine them to create an individualized, local element set or scheme that you will apply to your specific digital collection. In some situations, you may also choose to define local metadata elements that are not drawn from an existing standard, if none of the standard elements meets your particular need. For example, if you are using the Dublin Core element set, none of the fifteen fields may be specific enough to describe a certain aspect of a resource (although utilizing refinements in this instance may also be a suitable solution).

At this point you may be asking, how do I decide which elements to select for my particular scheme? Your choice may be influenced in part by the software you have chosen to deliver your digital content online, since a given system may support only a select few metadata standards (although this limitation can also be dealt with by mapping from one metadata standard to another, as discussed later on). In general, though, you will want to base your scheme on a core set of elements that complements the type of resources you are describing and addresses the needs of your users. A general-purpose element set such as Dublin Core may be suitable for a collection of resources in various formats that are intended for the general public. At the other end of the spectrum, a specific type of resource or community of users may require a more specialized element set; for example, an archivist wanting to create online, searchable finding aids for researchers would naturally opt for EAD, while a museum curator describing digital versions of artwork for scholars would be likely to have his or her needs best met by VRA Core. There are many such domain-specific standards that are geared toward various communities and data types, from education and social sciences to moving images and geospatial data sets.

As is the case with most other topics in this book, metadata scheme design is not a one-size-fits-all process; it will vary depending on the needs of the individual institution and the types of digital content that the scheme will cover. Once you have selected and developed your element set, there are certain decisions that you will need to make concerning each element in your scheme. These include the following:

- Will the element be required or optional for each metadata record?
- Will the element be repeatable within each metadata record, or will it only be allowed once?
- Will the metadata field and its associated value be visible in the public display of the metadata record? Certain types of technical and admin-

istrative metadata may be suppressed from public view and only be visible to the metadata creator who is logged into the system interface.
- What field name will the metadata element display in the public record? For example, for a collection of photographs you may substitute the Dublin Core term *Creator* with *Photographer* in the public display.

Another important decision that you will need to make for each element is whether the value should adhere to any particular content specification. For example, must the value be taken from a specified thesaurus or controlled vocabulary, or must it be formatted according to a data content standard like AACR or DACS? Must dates or codes be formatted according to a certain standard? You may specify different data value or content standards for each element in your scheme.

It is common to assign a data content standard to an element like *Title* so that the metadata creator will have specific guidelines to follow in structuring the value—rules dictating, for example, what words should be capitalized and whether or not leading articles such as *an* or *the* should be included. Data value standards, or controlled vocabularies, are generally assigned to elements for which it is important to maintain strict consistency in the values of these elements across multiple records. This consistency is crucial for successful search and browse functionalities. Elements that typically require controlled vocabularies include *Subject, Name, Location,* and *Type*. Similarly, *Date* and *Language* elements will generally follow an encoding schema indicating how these values should be constructed. Dates commonly follow the format *yyyy-mm-dd,* as computers are unable to process date values that are not strictly numerical.

There are multiple controlled vocabularies and thesauri to choose from, and in selecting one, you will want to consider the type of content you are describing as well as the community of users who will be using your collection. For a collection of library or archival materials, you may want to use the vocabularies that are created and maintained by the Library of Congress, including LCSH, the Library of Congress Name Authority File (LCNAF), and the Library of Congress Thesaurus for Graphic Materials (LCTGM). For museum materials, you may be more likely to select the Getty Research Institute's offerings, which include the AAT, the Union List of Artist Names (ULAN), and the Getty Thesaurus of Geographic Names (TGN).

In selecting a controlled vocabulary for a specific element, you may decide that the available vocabularies do not meet your needs. This may be the case if you are working with a collection in which none of the associated names or locations appears in an established authority file because they are not widely known. In this instance, you may decide to create your own controlled vocabulary containing local terms for names, places, subjects, or other values. While this process may represent a significant undertaking for a large institution or consortium that wishes to construct a detailed local vocabulary, for the smaller institution it may mean merely compiling a simple list of local terms.

Similarly, you may decide to develop your own set of data content specifications or input guidelines. This can take the form of a simple set of guidelines for how to format values for metadata fields that do not have an associated controlled vocabulary or encoding scheme. In most cases you will want to follow an established content standard like AACR2, DACS, or CCO, but you may also wish to record some local content guidelines as well. These guidelines may be assigned at the collection level or the individual element level.

Documenting Your Metadata Scheme

Once you have designed your metadata scheme, it is crucial to create documentation outlining the decisions you've made and the best practices you've established. This document should spell out clearly what specifications are to be applied to each element in the scheme, so that metadata creators can use it to guide their content creation. Typically, you will want to include information such as the following for each element: the field label to be displayed in the metadata record; whether the element is required or repeatable; whether a controlled vocabulary or other encoding scheme should be used for the element value, and which one; and any local content guidelines that apply. You may also wish to include example entries for each metadata element.

You may in fact wish to create two separate sets of documentation: one that provides general best practice guidelines that apply across all digital collections that you create, and individual documents that give detailed guidelines for each collection. For example, if you have established MODS as the core metadata standard to be used for all of your collections, it may be a good idea to create a detailed document outlining your specifications for each field in the MODS element set. For each individual collection, you may then create a smaller chart that includes only the particular MODS elements to be used for that collection, along with notes and examples that are specific to that collection. This latter type of documentation is often referred to as an *application profile* or *data dictionary*. An example application profile that shows selected metadata elements for a collection of digitized images of the author James Michener, taken by the photographer Robert Vavra, is presented in table 6.4 (pages 106–07). The metadata scheme for this collection is comprised solely of elements that map to Dublin Core, but a metadata scheme and its accompanying application profile can contain elements from multiple metadata standards.

Taken in tandem, a broad set of best practices guidelines along with collection-specific data dictionaries will provide metadata creators with the information they need to create consistent, quality metadata. These types of documents will also serve as important records for your institution. If you are working within a consortium or other large-scale collaborative group, you will likely be supplied with certain community-level best practices or member guidelines that have been previously established. These may be very specific or general and open to interpretation. Regardless, it is a good idea to also detail your local practices at the project level in the form of a data dictionary or similar document.

Metadata Interoperability

An important concept to keep in mind when designing your metadata scheme is the idea of *interoperability*. In a nutshell, interoperability refers to the ability of multiple systems to exchange data with minimal loss of information and functionality. With so many different metadata standards out there, you may wonder how useful your metadata or another institution's metadata will be if it is taken out of its local context. For example, you may decide you want to share your metadata with an outside repository, or merge records with those from another collection that uses a different scheme. Perhaps at some point in the future, you will decide to migrate your digital collections to a different software platform or online system—will this new system be able to ingest and use metadata from your current scheme, including locally created elements? It's also possible that in the future, you will decide that a different metadata standard is preferable to the one you're using and that you need to convert your existing metadata into a different format (for example, from Dublin Core to MODS).

Cases such as these will generally involve a process known as *mapping*, in which metadata from one element set or scheme is converted to another. Mapping is usually facilitated by the creation of a *crosswalk*, a table or other visual representation that shows how elements from two or more different schemes correlate with each other. A simplified crosswalk, showing the mapping of selected top-level elements between Dublin Core and MODS, is given in table 6.5 (page 108). Many metadata standards have previously developed crosswalks which are available on their respective websites.

Mapping between metadata schemes generally results in some loss of information. The extent to which one element set may be mapped successfully to another is dependent on the similarity of the schemes. If one scheme is significantly simpler than the other, if the elements in one are more granular, or if the content standards used to create the element values are not compatible, then there is likely to be a greater loss of information in the conversion of one to the other. Likewise, it may prove somewhat problematic if you are mapping from a set of locally created metadata elements to a more generic element set like Dublin Core, which may not contain an exact match for certain elements that are specific to the local set. For these reasons, it is generally a good idea to keep future interoperability in mind when designing a metadata scheme, and to give careful thought to your choice of standards.

TABLE 6.4
Application profile example: *Robert Vavra Photographs* digital collection

Field Label	Mapped to Dublin Core Element	Controlled Vocabulary/ Encoding Schema	Required?	Format/Input Guidelines	Example Entries
Title	Title		Yes	Brief description of image, with subject names and locations if known	James A. Michener watching the running of the bulls in Pamplona, Spain
Photographer	Creator	Library of Congress Name Authority File (LCNAF)	Yes, if known	Use name form established in LCNAF when present. When not, use the format *last name, first name*, and add middle name or initial, date of birth and/or date of death, if known.	Vavra, Robert Fulton, John, 1933–1998
Type of Resource	Type	Dublin Core Metadata Initiative Type Vocabulary (DCMIType)	Yes	All items in collection will have value *Still image*.	Still image
Digital Image Publisher	Publisher		Yes	Entity responsible for publication of digital image	University of Northern Colorado Libraries. Archival Services Department
Date Created	Date.Created	International Organization for Standardization time and date format (ISO 8601)	Yes, if known	Use the format *yyyy-mm-dd* when specific dates are known. If exact year, month, or day is not known, give a probable date range or decade. Add a question mark for uncertain but probable dates.	1965-06-01 1965–1968 1960s 1965?
Original Size	Format. Extent		Yes, if known	Size of original photograph or negative	4 × 5 inches 6 × 6 cm

Original Form	Format. Medium	Art and Architecture Thesaurus (AAT)	Yes	Form of original analog resource	Negatives (photographic) Black-and-white photographs
Digital File Format	Format	Internet Media Type (MIME)	Yes	The file format of the digital image	image/jpeg image/gif
Topics	Subject	Library of Congress Subject Headings (LCSH); AAT	Yes	Primary topics/subjects depicted in image	Bulls (animals) Festivals Fiesta de San Fermin
People	Subject	LCNAF	No	Person depicted in the image. Follow input guidelines for *Photographer*, above.	Michener, James A. (James Albert), 1907–1997 Ordóñez Araujo, Antonio, 1932–1998
Places	Coverage. Spatial	LCNAF	No	Location depicted in the image	Pamplona (Spain)
Local Identifier	Identifier		Yes	Identifier assigned to digital file, following format *Collection#_series#_item#*	JM041_02_0022
Original Collection	Relation. IsPartOf		Yes	Name of original archival collection in which physical materials are located	James A. Michener Papers, Robert Vavra photographs and correspondence JM041, Series 2: Photographs and Negatives
Digital Collection	Relation. IsPartOf		Yes	Name of digital collection of which the image is a part	Robert Vavra Photographs Digital Collection
Copyright Statement	Rights		Yes	Information about rights restrictions/copyright status of item	Copyright belongs to the University of Northern Colorado.

TABLE 6.5
Sample metadata crosswalk: Dublin Core to MODS

Unqualified Dublin Core Elements	MODS Elements
Title	titleInfo
Creator	name
Contributor	name
Type	typeOfResource
Date	originInfo
Publisher	originInfo
Relation	relatedItem
Rights	accessRestriction

Final Thoughts

Metadata for digital collections is an extremely complex topic, and this chapter is intended only to introduce you to basic ideas and a common vocabulary to aid you in further study. Before you begin putting this information into practice, you may want to spend time exploring the topic further by looking at metadata records for various digital collections online and considering how the metadata designer made decisions about such aspects as standards and level of granularity. There are also many organizations that have produced guidelines or best practices guides for metadata creation, and you may choose to adapt some of these for your own needs. Some examples include the Mountain West Digital Library Dublin Core Application Profile (MWDL 2011) and the Digital Library Foundation/Aquifer Guidelines for Shareable MODS Records (DLF Aquifer Metadata Working Group 2009).

Above all, keep in mind that working with metadata is as much an art as it is a science. Just as there is not a universal metadata standard, there is not necessarily a "right" way to create a metadata scheme for your digital collections. Much depends on personal judgment and a careful consideration of the individual collection, the needs of your users, and accepted norms and best practices of the particular community.

RESOURCES

DLF Aquifer Metadata Working Group. 2009. "Digital Library Federation/Aquifer Implementation Guidelines for Shareable MODS Records." https://wiki.dlib.indiana.edu/download/attachments/24288/DLFMODS_ImplementationGuidelines.pdf.

Gilliland, Anne J. 2008. "Setting the Stage." In *Introduction to Metadata: Online Edition, Version 3.0,* edited by Murtha Baca. Los Angeles: Getty Research Institute. www.getty.edu/research/publications/electronic_publications/intrometadata/setting.html.

Miller, Paul. 2004. "Metadata: What It Means for Memory Institutions." In *Metadata Applications and Management,* edited by G. E. Gorman and Daniel G. Dorner, 4–16. Lanham, MD: Scarecrow.

Miller, Steven J. 2011. *Metadata for Digital Collections: A How-to-Do-It Manual.* New York: Neal-Schuman.

Mountain West Digital Library (MWDL). 2011. "Mountain West Digital Library Dublin Core Application Profile." http://mwdl.org/docs/MWDL_DC_Profile_Version_2.0.pdf.

NISO (National Information Standards Organization). 2013. *The Dublin Core Element Set.* Baltimore, MD: NISO. www.niso.org/apps/group_public/download.php/10256/Z39-85- 2012_dublin_core.pdf.

Phillips, Jennifer. 2013. "Learning about Metadata." In *Jump-Start Your Career as a Digital Librarian: A LITA Guide,* edited by Jane Monson, 131–32. Chicago: American Library Association.

Puglia, Steven, Jeffrey Reed, and Erin Rhodes. 2004. "Technical Guidelines for Digitizing Archival Materials for Electronic Access: Creation of Production Master Files—Raster Images," p. 8. National Archives and Records Administration. www.archives.gov/research_room/arc/arc_info/techguide_raster_june2004.pdf.

Riley, Jenn. 2009. "Seeing Standards: A Visualization of the Metadata Universe." www.dlib.indiana.edu/~jenlrile/metadatamap.

Zeng, Marcia Lei and Jian Qin. 2016. *Metadata.* 2nd edition. Chicago: ALA Neal-Schuman.

DIGITAL COLLECTION MANAGEMENT SYSTEMS

A CRUCIAL STEP IN DEVELOPING YOUR DIGITIZATION program is choosing and implementing an online system for organizing and managing your digital assets and delivering them to end users—in fact, the success and viability of your digital projects can be highly dependent on this decision.

These systems are single software solutions that generally offer the following core functionalities: capture, storage, and retrieval of digital content; back-end tools for cataloging and managing the content; and front-end tools for displaying, searching, and browsing the content (some systems also offer tools for preserving content). At its most basic, the core architecture of these systems consists of an underlying database for storage, an indexing application for search and retrieval, and user interfaces for interacting with content. Beyond that, these systems may vary greatly in their levels of sophistication, ranging from basic to cutting-edge. Some software packages can either be customized to a high degree, or simply installed out-of-the-box with few adjustments. When browsing various institutions' digital collections online you will likely see the same underlying systems used over and over again, but you may see marked differences in their appearance depending on the amount of development and customization the institution has applied.

These types of systems may be known by different names, including *content management system, digital asset management system,* or *digital repository system.* While the names are often used interchangeably, there may be subtle differences between each of these types of content platforms. "Content management system," or CMS, is an umbrella term that can generally be used to describe a wide range of applications that allow users to publish, edit, and organize digital content of all types—WordPress, Drupal, and Joomla! are some well-known and popular all-purpose CMSs that are often used by web developers to create websites of all kinds. Digital asset management systems, or DAMS, are commonly associated with the commercial sector (often media organizations) and may be used internally within an organization to store and organize digital content (although they may also be used to share content externally via a public interface). Digital repository systems are usually associated with academic and nonprofit institutions, and are often used as the infrastructure for what one might consider a typical "digital library" in the sense of an online extension of an information organization. They are typically developed and marketed specifically for libraries and other cultural heritage institutions, and are developed in accordance with established library, archive, and museum standards. Since there is a great deal of overlap among these different types of systems, for the purposes of this book we will use the general-purpose term *digital collection management system,* or DCMS for short, when referring to any kind of software used to store, manage, and deliver digital content.

Some institutions with the necessary resources available, including sufficient funding and dedicated programmers on staff, will create their own digital collection software from scratch, as this allows them greater control over their system and the ability to customize it exactly to their needs. Most institutions don't have the resources to do this, and will follow one of two models: either license a commercial product or use a freely available open source platform. Each of these routes has its pros and cons, and the decision to follow one or the other is highly dependent on the situation of the individual institution. Before choosing a DCMS, it's a good idea to take the time to thoroughly research all your options. There are many factors to consider in this process, and these will be covered in more detail later in the chapter. For now, we will start with a brief overview of some commonly used products in the cultural heritage community.

DCMS Options

As mentioned previously, there are generally two options when it comes to digital collections management software: *proprietary* and *open source*. Proprietary, or commercial, systems are owned and licensed by a vendor that controls the computer code underlying the system (in other words, the code can be considered "closed source"). Customers are effectively leasing the product, and in return for a yearly licensing fee they receive what is basically a turnkey, out-of-the-box solution that includes dedicated technical support. Proprietary options are usually relatively easy to implement, since the vendor does most of the heavy lifting in terms of setting up and customizing the software, hosting it on a cloud-based server, troubleshooting problems, and providing periodic software upgrades. Thus, they are a good choice for institutions that do not have sufficient IT resources to host and manage their own systems.

Open source repository platforms, in contrast, are openly available on the Internet and can generally be downloaded and used without a fee. While open source software is not by definition free of charge, as programmers can charge money for the code they create, most open source licenses require that the source code be made freely available when the software is sold or distributed. In practice, especially in the cultural heritage community, open source software is commonly free to download and use. The source code may be modified by users to suit their individual needs, and users that make changes to the code may share these back with the open source community. Depending on how active the user community is, open source programs may be in a constant state of flux, with new functionalities and improvements being made available as they are created by users.

In recent years, the line between proprietary and open source systems has started to become less defined as new service models emerge. Third-party vendors now offer commercial support for institutions using an open source DCMS, ranging from à la carte hourly technical support for locally installed software to full-service packages that include cloud-based software hosting and ongoing maintenance. Thus, it is possible to combine many of the benefits of proprietary and open source systems in a single software solution. These benefits will be discussed in detail later in the chapter.

There are too many DCMS options on the market to cover them all in a single chapter. Here we will look at some of the more well-established platforms that are widely used in the cultural heritage community. There are certainly other products available, and the fact that they are not included in this chapter should not be taken as a criticism of their quality. It's entirely possible that a lesser-known or more specialized system will meet your institution's needs better than the ones mentioned below, and it is recommended that you research options beyond those listed. However, these represent a good cross-section of the current DCMS market, ranging from basic to cutting-edge.

Proprietary Software Options

CONTENTDM

Within the library community, CONTENTdm (www.contentdm.org) is one of the major players in commercial DCMS software. A product of OCLC, it can be licensed as a hosted service or it can be installed on an institution's own server and managed by local system administrators. CONTENTdm is a well-established product, having originated in the late 1990s at the University of Washington, and is currently on its sixth version. It has been widely adopted by cultural heritage, education, and government organizations. The software provides robust support for image, audio, and video files, and is therefore commonly used to deliver collections of digitized special collections and archival materials such as photographs, maps, oral histories, and film clips.

The CONTENTdm platform allows users to create metadata using Dublin Core, VRA Core, and METS, and there are nine controlled vocabularies and thesauri that are built into the system, including the Art & Architecture Thesaurus, Dublin Core Metadata Initiative Type Vocabulary, and Getty Thesaurus of Geographic Names. Users can also customize metadata templates for individual collections. Various extensions to the system are available, including one that uses OCR to create searchable full-text transcripts from image files. CONTENTdm is a popular choice for collaborative digital projects because multiple organizations can store their collections on distributed drives. For institutions that already subscribe to other OCLC products such as WorldCat Discovery Services, a "quick start" hosted instance of CONTENTdm is available at no additional charge; however, it is limited to one hundred objects. While this may prove useful for evaluation purposes or for institutions with very small collections, it is likely to be too limiting for the needs of most institutions in running an actual production site.

DIGITAL COMMONS

A second proprietary system that is widely used in the library community is Digital Commons (http://digitalcommons.bepress.com). Digital Commons is a product of bepress, a company that arose out of a project at the University of California, Berkeley, in the late 1990s. Digital Commons is designed to be used for a type of digital library known as an *institutional repository*. Institutional repositories, or IRs, are most closely associated with academic and other research institutions and can be described as "digital archive[s] of the intellectual product created by the faculty, research staff, and students of an institution" (Crow 2002). IRs tend to focus on the collection and preservation of research outputs, such as journal articles published by faculty and electronic theses and dissertations (ETDs) created by students. While IRs are generally more narrow in scope than other types of digital libraries, and tend to focus heavily on the collection of text files such as pdfs, systems designed for IRs typically support other file types including image, audio, and video. Therefore, they can be used to deliver all manner of digital collections, and this can be seen more commonly with open source IR software that may be customized for use with more traditional archival image collections.

In the case of Digital Commons, the system is heavily marketed for IRs and is licensed almost exclusively by institutions that use it for that purpose. The software offers functionalities that are specific to the needs of researchers, such as the ability to place temporary embargoes on content (this may be required by journal publishers or preferred by students who hope to publish their ETDs in article or book form in the future). The system features workflows that allow contributors to upload their own files and metadata to the repository and provides metrics for them to track when and where their content is being downloaded. Digital Commons can also be used as a journal publishing platform, a feature that sets it apart from other DCMSs. Since the interface is designed primarily for displaying text files and metadata, browsing image-heavy collections can be difficult. For these reasons, Digital Commons is not an obvious choice for institutions that wish to display mainly image collections, although it is an option for such uses. It is common for academic institutions to use a platform like Digital Commons for their IR and a separate platform like CONTENTdm for their image collections, taking advantage of the strengths of each type of system.

PASTPERFECT

While CONTENTdm and Digital Commons are geared largely toward libraries, there are other types of DCMSs that are tailored more for the needs of museums, historical societies, and archives. One such system is PastPerfect (www.museumsoftware.com), a commercial software that has been on the market since 1996 and is now in its fifth version. PastPerfect is primarily a collection management system that is widely used by museums and similar organizations to catalog their holdings. The basic software provides tools for managing tasks that are specific to these types of organizations, such as tracking and recording accessions, loans, exhibits, and information about donors and members. In order to create digital collections that can be shared publicly online, PastPerfect users must purchase "add-ons" or upgrades that allow them to attach digital multimedia files to their catalog records and then share these files and records on the Web. With the digital collections add-on, subscribers receive web design assistance and have the option of paying an annual fee for file hosting. A separate virtual exhibit add-on allows users to create structured online exhibits of selected digital objects; this feature lacks the search and browse capabilities of the digital collections add-on.

PastPerfect may be a good option for cultural heritage institutions that are already using the basic software package to manage their physical holdings, as the software can merely be extended to accommodate online delivery of digital collections. Compared with other commercial systems, it is a relatively affordable product that does not require annual licensing fees. It is meant to be a straightforward, out-of-the-box solution that requires little in the way of technical or web expertise. For these reasons, PastPerfect is appropriate for organizations with small budgets and staff that desire a simple, turnkey solution. At the same time, the software was not developed primarily for managing and displaying digital assets, so it lacks the sophistication of products that were designed expressly for this purpose. Institutions should think carefully about whether such a system will continue to meet their needs over time as their digital collections grow in complexity, and be prepared for the eventuality of migrating their content to a more robust DCMS.

LUNA

LUNA (formerly Luna Insight) is a DCMS that is geared toward the delivery of digital image collections, and for this reason it is well-suited for organizations that deal in visual resources, such as art museums and academic institutions with large visual resource collections. The LUNA software is a product of Luna Imaging, a California-based company that also offers digital imaging services for cultural heritage institutions (www.lunaimaging.com/). Customers can arrange to have the company both scan and upload their digitized materials into the LUNA system, which may be an appealing solution for those with few staff to complete those activities on-site. Site licenses are available so that software can be installed on local servers, with various levels of accompanying technical support offered, and a hosted service includes technical support bundled in. Additional tools can be added on to the base software that are intended to facilitate cross-institutional collection building within a consortium. LUNA SOLO is a low-cost version of the software that is available as a monthly subscription and is marketed for individual users rather than institutions, and this could also be an option for institutions wishing to host very small collections.

LUNA supports Dublin Core and VRA Core natively, and users may create their own metadata templates from scratch. Local authorities and controlled vocabularies can also be imported into the system. The capability that LUNA provides for interacting with images may be its most appealing feature for many subscribers; it has a sophisticated image viewer interface and users can add images to a "workspace" that provides advanced tools for manipulating multiple images simultaneously. Registered users can also create "media groups" of personalized image collections that can be shared via a custom URL or web widget. Additionally, LUNA includes some functionality that is not commonly found in other DCMS solutions, including the ability to build presentations and slide shows from selected content and the integration of e-commerce services that allow users to purchase images directly from the site.

Open Source Software Options

GREENSTONE

There is a wide spectrum of open source DCMS options, and in general, you will find the widest variety of products and most active software development happening in this area. One of the oldest open source digital library systems is Greenstone, developed in the late 1990s at the University of Waikato in New Zealand. The software is now in its second major iteration, Greenstone3, having been completely redesigned and updated from its original version. Greenstone is unique among similar projects in that it has evolved to have a strong international and humanitarian focus. In fact, it is developed and distributed by the New Zealand Digital Library Project in cooperation with UNESCO and a nongovernmental organization based in Belgium called Human Info. According to its website, "the aim of the Greenstone software is to empower users, particularly in universities, libraries, and other public service institutions, to build their own digital libraries" (www.greenstone.org/ "About Greenstone"). In keeping with its international focus, the software's user interface is available in over sixty languages.

The Greenstone project has a particular emphasis on helping organizations in the developing world to produce and distribute their own digital library collections. Because it caters to users with low-level technology skills, it can be a good choice for small organizations without much IT support. Out-of-the-box, it provides a fairly bare-bones user interface. However, the system is configurable and can be customized to look and feel like a more sophisticated product. It supports a variety of metadata formats including Dublin Core, and can ingest and display most common file formats. In a nutshell, Greenstone is a good basic DCMS that can be implemented and managed relatively easily; however, some web design expertise is required to give the interface a modern and attractive appearance.

DSPACE

While Greenstone is an example of a DCMS that is used most commonly for the management and delivery of archival collections, in the world of open source, much energy has been directed toward the development of systems that are designed specifically to be used as IRs. This makes sense, given that the trend for establishing IRs at many universities and other institutions has been driven in large part by a desire to maintain control over locally produced assets, rather than handing ownership over to commercial publishers. (In the academic library world, this is closely tied to the "serials crisis," whereby the scholarly publishing marketplace has been distorted to the point that many libraries can hardly afford to purchase the journals in which their own institutionally funded research is published.) The effort to achieve greater open access of institutional research outputs dovetails closely with the open source software movement, with its emphasis on transparency.

The most popular open source software for IRs is DSpace, which was developed as a collaborative project between the Massachusetts Institute of Technology and Hewlett-Packard Labs and first released in 2002 (it is now in its sixth version). Members of the DSpace project team have defined the system as "a dynamic repository for the intellectual output in digital formats of multidisciplinary research organizations" (Smith et al. 2003). It is intended to be a turnkey IR platform that institutions can install and operate with a minimum of technical expertise. At the same time, like all open source software it is highly customizable, so users with the appropriate programming skills can modify and improve the system to meet their institution's specific needs. With its active user community, many such developers have created "extensions" that add expanded functionality to the base software—some of these are available to download for free, while others must be purchased from third-party vendors. Many of these vendors also offer consulting services that may include hosting, installation, and site design and customization.

The DSpace website at www.dspace.org provides a wealth of information including user guides and online training materials, a wiki, a link to a demo site for testing the software, lists of registered service providers, and a user registry featuring hundreds of examples of DSpace repositories from around the world. The user registry is dominated by academic institutions, but you will also find a significant number of government, nonprofit, museum, and even commercial users on the list, demonstrating that the software can be customized for a variety of purposes beyond the academic IR. The system supports all manner of digital formats and uses Dublin Core as its default metadata schema, but other standard schemas may be added to the system's "metadata registry" and custom schemas may be created as well. DSpace also provides tools for supporting digital preservation, such as a built-in fixity checker for verifying checksums (see chapter 9 for more on digital preservation and a discussion of checksums).

FEDORA

DSpace is closely associated with another open source DCMS, Fedora (www.fedora-commons.org). The two systems were developed separately and were overseen by their respective nonprofit organizations, the DSpace Foundation and Fedora Commons, until 2009, when these entities joined to form a collaborative project called DuraSpace (www.duraspace.org). DuraSpace now oversees both DSpace and Fedora, in addition to other projects such as the cloud-based, hosted archiving service DuraCloud, mentioned in chapter 9. DuraSpace also offers a DSpace hosting service, DSpaceDirect.

Though they are closely linked and can be used for many of the same purposes, DSpace and Fedora differ in important ways. Fedora, which stands for "Flexible Extensible Digital Object Repository Architecture," originated at Cornell University in 1997, became a joint project of Cornell and the University of Virginia in 2001, and was first released in 2003. What sets Fedora apart from other digital content management systems is that it functions primarily as a management layer for digital objects, which can be used as a framework for creating a variety of different types of repositories. In other words, Fedora is more an architecture or infrastructure that uses a modular approach and web services, rather than an out-of-the-box repository solution (Calhoun 2014). Fedora is meant to act as a "foundation layer" upon which various types of systems and applications can be built; according to Lagoze et al., "this distinguishes Fedora from other complex object systems that are turnkey, vertical applications for storing and manipulating complex objects through a fixed user interface," such as DSpace and Greenstone (2006).

All of this is to say that Fedora is not a straightforward, prepackaged repository system that can be downloaded and implemented easily. It is a powerful system that offers especially strong support for digital preservation, providing functionalities like persistent identifiers, versioning, and checksums (covered in chapter 9). But working directly with the software can be complex because it requires some understanding of the abstract data model on which the architecture is modeled. And, importantly for institutions that wish to share their digital collections online, it provides only a very basic interface for interacting with the digital objects stored in the system. In and of itself, Fedora is not a very accessible solution for smaller organizations lacking in web development and programming expertise. However, Fedora serves as the foundation for a new generation of open source digital repositories that have the advantage of being highly modular and flexible, allowing for a greater degree of customization at the individual repository level.

ISLANDORA

One such system is Islandora (http://islandora.ca). The name alludes to the fact that the software was originally created at the University of Prince Edward Island; it is now being actively developed by an international open source community. Islandora is built upon a number of open source applications, primarily Fedora and the popular CMS Drupal, which can be used as a framework for websites of various kinds. Drupal provides the front-end layer for Islandora, allowing for the creation of attractive and user-friendly interfaces for displaying digital objects and metadata, something Fedora on its own lacks. Drupal also allows for customizable metadata entry forms and supports all metadata standards, including custom schemas. Fedora itself forms the underlying digital object repository layer, where digital objects and metadata are stored along with security policies for access and management. The integration of Drupal and Fedora allows for the separation of the data layer and the interface layer, making the platform highly modular. A third code layer combines various other open source applications that provide functionalities such as image conversion and OCR. The system can be extended further by enabling "solution packs" that provide additional features and support for different object formats.

One of the benefits of Islandora is that it takes a complex but powerful software like Fedora and makes it more accessible to the average user. Another advantage that Islandora has over other open source repository systems is its flexibility. It can easily be used to host a research-heavy IR or a digital library of archival holdings such as photos, manuscripts, newspapers, and multimedia. It can even be configured to deliver both of these types of collections in the same system, which can be appealing for organizations that want to have both an IR and a digital image library, but can't or don't want to manage two separate systems. Islandora is also a popular choice for consortia and other group arrangements because multiple individual sites can be connected to a central repository. With such a "multi-site" configuration, a "root" Islandora installation serves as the basis for a number of offshoot sites which can be customized and managed by the site owners. This setup allows for the repository architecture to be shared across all sites while also permitting flexibility for individual organizations.

HYDRA

A similar approach to highly flexible, next-generation repository architecture can be found with the Hydra Project (http://projecthydra.org/). Hydra is one of the newer DCMS options, having started in 2008 as a collaboration between the University of Hull, Stanford University, the University of Virginia, and the organization that was then Fedora Commons (now DuraSpace). The initial goal of the Hydra Project was to create a "reusable framework [that] could be established for use with Fedora to enable multipurpose, multifunctional repository-enabled solutions for use across multiple institutions" (Awre and Cramer 2012). Like Islandora, the Hydra framework is built on a "technology stack" of multiple open source applications tied to a base Fedora installation.

The name Hydra alludes to the mythical serpent of Greek lore that has one body and many heads; similarly, a Hydra repository provides multiple points of access, or views, onto a common Fedora repository. Hydra "heads" are front-end applications developed for specific use cases, for example different content types, contexts, or user interactions. Examples of Hydra heads include those created for IRs, digital image libraries, multimedia libraries, and cataloging workflows. These tailored applications are shared with the Hydra community as "solution bundles," allowing other institutions to reuse, adapt, and modify them for their own needs. As of this writing, Hydra does not support out-of-the-box deployments, so the system is not suitable for institutions that desire a turnkey solution. However, the Hydra community is actively developing solution bundles, such as "Hydra-in-a-Box," that would enable users to easily install, configure, and maintain a local Hydra installation, or subscribe to a hosted service. This project is being funded by the Institute of Museum and Library Services with the aim of making Hydra a practical solution for libraries, archives, and museums of all sizes. A similar grant-funded project has also produced the Avalon Media System (www.avalonmediasystem.org), a Hydra-based open source DCMS for managing and delivering digital audio and video files.

OMEKA

Another next-generation open source system of note is Omeka (http://omeka.org). Omeka is a project of the Roy Rosenzweig Center for History and New Media at George Mason University and was first released in 2008. According to the Omeka website, the software falls at a crossroads of web content management systems like Drupal and Wordpress, library and archival repository and digital collections systems like DSpace and Fedora, and museum collection management and online exhibition systems like PastPerfect (CHNM 2016). Omeka is targeted equally to librarians, archivists, museum professionals, educators, and scholars who would like to create online collections and exhibits, but who lack the technical skills or resources to do so using other available systems. It is a popular product for academics conducting projects in the burgeoning field of digital humanities, which can be defined in a simplified sense as the use of digital tools for the study and teaching of humanities disciplines such as English and history. Omeka touts its five-minute installation, but it does require a LAMP (Linux, Apache, MySQL, PHP) setup to run on a local server. As Kucsma, Reiss, and Sidman observe, "For a user comfortable with setting up LAMP applications, an Omeka installation can be efficiently accomplished in a very short amount of time. For novice web developers installation may be more challenging" (2010). An alternative to local installation is the Omeka.net hosting service (www.omeka.net), which offers a variety of packages ranging from free to around $1,000 per year.

Omeka has a strong emphasis on display and offers a variety of prepackaged themes, or site designs, that users may choose from. This provides the advantage of professional-looking web design out-of-the-box; some themes even incorporate responsive web design, which adapts the site layout to the viewing environment, whether it be a desktop computer monitor or a mobile phone. Omeka is also highly flexible, and its core functionality may be extended with dozens of plug-ins that provide added features, such as an exhibit builder and map and time line creators. Omeka's default metadata is unqualified Dublin Core, but users may also import other metadata sets or create customized metadata vocabularies.

COLLECTIVEACCESS

Finally, it is worth mentioning another relative newcomer on the open source DCMS scene, CollectiveAccess, formerly known as OpenCollection (www.collectiveaccess.org). While often compared to Omeka, CollectiveAccess actually has more in common with PastPerfect in that it is a collections management system marketed for museums, archives, and special collections that provides an additional front-end tool for delivering digital collections online. While Omeka is oriented toward the creation of discrete online projects, CollectiveAccess can be considered more of an enterprise-level solution for management and discovery. It offers a full range of cataloging and collections management features as part of its core back-end module, including support for multilingual cataloging and metadata standards such as Dublin Core, VRA Core, and EAD; tools to generate finding aids; and support for loan tracking, exhibition management, and conservation and inventory workflows. An optional front-end module allows for the creation of a public-access web portal for showcasing configurable galleries that can incorporate value-added features like time lines, maps, and other visualization tools.

Setting up CollectiveAccess to deliver digital collections requires installing both software modules on a local server, and the installation process is somewhat more complicated than Omeka's. The CollectiveAccess development team offers consulting services that include cloud hosting packages and data migration. As a newer product, CollectiveAccess offers a more sophisticated and robust digital collections user interface than PastPerfect. However, like PastPerfect, delivery of digital collections is not the primary function of the software, and unlike Omeka it is not an obvious choice for creating one-off digital exhibits. The larger scope of the system requires a greater commitment of the user, but it can be an excellent open source solution for combining collections management with delivery of digital collections.

Evaluating and Choosing a DCMS

Selecting a DCMS for storing, managing, and delivering your digital collections is not a decision to be taken lightly. Considerable thought should be given to the task and the available solutions weighed in order to ensure that you are choosing the system that best meets your individual needs. Making an uninformed decision may result in the need to migrate your content to a more suitable platform in the not-too-distant future; while this may be unavoidable in the long term as systems evolve, it can be a costly and time-consuming exercise that you will want to avoid whenever possible. The following section outlines some factors to consider when comparing the different DCMS options that are available.

OPEN SOURCE VS. PROPRIETARY SYSTEMS

One of the most important aspects of choosing a DCMS is deciding whether to use an open source or a proprietary product. Neither type is inherently better than the other, but there are pros and cons to each that need to be clearly understood. For example, it is easy to make the assumption that open source systems are the most cost-effective solution, since the software is typically free to use. However, there can be a number of hidden costs associated with open source software. It's important to consider the total cost of ownership, or TCO, of a system, which can be defined as the direct and indirect costs throughout its entire life cycle (Samuels and Griffy 2012). Though it may have a low up-front cost, the TCO for an open source system can be just as substantial as for a proprietary one when other aspects are factored in, such as fixing software problems, purchasing and maintaining servers, or paying hosting fees. And while often costly in terms of annual licensing fees, a proprietary system can save an institution money in staff time and equipment costs.

Depending on the specific situation of an institution, both open source and proprietary systems may end up balancing each other out financially. If your institution already has a strong technology infrastructure in place, including staff with the expertise to install, customize, and manage the system, as well as dedicated server space for storing and delivering files, then open source software can be a fairly low-cost option. For organizations that lack these assets, using an open source system may require purchasing new server equipment, hiring a programmer or web developer to set up and customize the system, or paying a third-party service to host and maintain the software. If you are able to install an open source system locally, the up-front costs of setting it up may be offset by savings in hosting fees over time. If you pay an annual fee to have an open source system hosted, your cost savings may not be significant compared with a proprietary system. While not an easy task, your institution should attempt to assess the long-term costs of a system beyond the initial purchase price; these will be highly dependent upon local factors that are tied to available resources.

That being said, there are often instances when one type of DCMS is clearly better suited to a particular organization's needs than another. For small institutions, a proprietary system may be a clear choice, and the main point of deliberation may be deciding which one to purchase. The chief advantage of a proprietary DCMS is that it provides a turnkey solution—the customer generally has no software to install and update or servers to maintain and back up, and technical support is usually included. With these systems, what you see is typically what you get, with the exception of having the ability to make cosmetic changes to the user interface design. This ease of use is a deciding factor for many institutions, and rightly so. Many institutions also find that the technical support they receive from a vendor, which can include not just software maintenance and troubleshooting but assistance with content migration and metadata customization, is well worth the cost.

While proprietary systems work well for institutions that desire a high level of professional support built in, for others, the factors that tip the balance in favor of open source software are autonomy and flexibility. In a survey of forty-nine libraries that had migrated or were in the process of migrating to a new DCMS, Stein and Thompson found that the majority of those that started with a proprietary system moved to an open source one (2015). Reasons given included a desire for greater flexibility in the range of file formats and metadata schemes supported and the extent to which the system could be customized and made more extensible (i.e., through the use of modules and plug-ins). Open source software offers the ability for an institution to exercise greater local control over its DCMS; this is especially appealing for those that have programmers and web developers available to modify the source code or design custom plug-ins. Many institutions also value the fact that with an open source system there is less danger that the product will be discontinued or otherwise cease to be supported, as sometimes occurs with commercial vendors. Cervone recommends one way to address this risk when licensing proprietary systems, suggesting that "it is always a good idea to have a clause in your license that guarantees the software will be put into escrow to protect you against the untimely demise of your vendor" (2006). These concerns and Cervone's advice can also be applied to third-party hosting of open source systems.

As the Stein and Thompson survey illustrates, your choice in DCMS need not be set in stone forever. While platform migration can be a protracted endeavor that should not be undertaken lightly, switching to a different system that better suits your needs is always an option. While in most cases you will want to be reasonably sure that the system you select will serve you in the long term, there are instances when it may make sense to strategically plan for short-term use. For example, Corbett et al. describe how Northeastern University used a proprietary system (Digital Commons) as a temporary location for their IR during the time that a local Fedora-based repository system was being developed (2016). Since the development process took two full years, the commercial system provided them with a suitable intermediary solution.

EVALUATING YOUR OPTIONS

Taking the time to complete a thorough comparison of the available systems is an important step in making an informed decision about the best DCMS for your situation. Some in the library community have documented best practices and methodologies for others to use in this process. Samuels and Griffy emphasize the importance of first establishing a set of system requirements which outline what the application is expected to accomplish (2012). For example, you may decide you want a system that supports the MODS metadata standard, will integrate with other specific software such as your library catalog or collection management system, and will allow administrators to set up workflows for approving content after upload. Your requirements will depend on the needs of your individual institution, but table 7.1 (page 128) provides a list of important factors to consider when developing your requirement set.

Your requirements should be established not only by a careful evaluation of your institution's needs, but also those of your users. Identifying your audience is critical, and clarifying the chosen audience enables assessment of their needs (DeRidder 2007). Consider the age range, education level, and technological sophistication of your user base. What will they be using your collections for, and what will their requirements be for navigating the system? A historical society whose largest audience is members of the public conducting genealogy research may need to tailor its system for a slightly different set of functionalities than a college library that is making its institution's scholarly output available for use mainly by students, faculty, and other researchers.

In establishing your requirements, you will also need to make decisions about which ones are essential and which ones may need to be put off for later or given up altogether. It's highly unlikely that any single DCMS will be able to meet all of your institution's preferred requirements, so you may need to make some hard choices about how critical each requirement is. Even if you determine that a system meets most of your needs, there will likely be certain functionalities that it does not support. In this situation, consider whether the particular function could be implemented another way or added on later (Cervone 2006). If the answer is no, you will have to weigh whether or not you can live without it.

TABLE 7.1
Factors to consider in DCMS evaluation

Metadata Creation	What metadata standards does the system support? Does it support certain controlled vocabularies or subject taxonomies? How easily can metadata schemas be customized?
Content Management	What file formats does the system accept? Does it support batch uploading? What is the process for migrating content into and out of the system? How easily can the system scale to support higher content volume and greater use?
End-User Functionalities	Is the user interface easy to navigate and use? What search functions are available (e.g., full-text, keyword)? How well does the interface display on different types and sizes of screens? Does the system allow the user to interact with the content (e.g., submit content, add tags to metadata, create personal collections, or share content on social media)?
Administrator Functionalities	Can administrators create workflows for tracking and managing content prior to publishing it? Can users be assigned roles that control what actions they are allowed to take in the system? Is the administrative interface easy to use?
Site Customization	To what extent can the user interface design be customized, and what skills are needed to do so? Can the system be extended with modules or plug-ins for additional functionality? Can it be integrated with other library systems?
Access Control	Can the system be integrated with a local authentication system such as LDAP or Shibboleth? Does it support IP and password controls? Can the system place embargoes on content or otherwise control levels of access to individual items or collections?
Preservation	Does the system support preservation functionalities such as checksums, versioning, or persistent identifiers?
Support	What sorts of training and documentation materials are available for system administrators? For open source systems, how active and helpful is the online user community? For proprietary or hosted systems, what level of technical support is provided by the vendor?

Deciding who to include in the evaluation process is another important consideration. You will want to consider involving people with expertise in the areas of cataloging or metadata, systems, archives, web development, and website usability. Obviously, this group would include whoever will be responsible for managing the system once it is established. Representation from IT staff is important if you are considering a locally hosted arrangement that will need to be installed and maintained on-site. If you are at an especially small institution, all of these areas of knowledge may not be represented on your staff. If that is the case, you may want to spend time reaching out to colleagues at other institutions who have undertaken this process and are willing to discuss their experiences with you. Professional e-mail lists in your field can also be a good place to seek advice, as people are often eager to share their opinions about various systems they have used. Just keep in mind that their experiences will be highly dependent on their specific institutional situations, which may not be generalizable to yours.

A crucial next step is to test your most promising software options in depth. If you have a long list of possible systems, use your required and preferred functionalities to narrow it down to a few that you will "test drive." Trying out a system is truly the best way to fully grasp its capabilities and limitations, and failure to do this can result in making an uninformed decision. If you are considering a proprietary system, the vendor should agree to allow you a trial period for testing the software. With open source systems, you will need to have the software installed on a local server for testing purposes. For those who lack the resources to do this, you may find that the system's website has an online "sandbox," or demo site, that you can use instead. If you're investigating an open source hosted solution, then the vendor may also be able to provide you with an online trial. Create a test collection in your test site and as you go through the various steps, assess such aspects as content upload, metadata creation and other workflows, and ease of using both the administrator and user interfaces.

It is a good idea to document your evaluation process in some fashion to ensure you are being consistent in your data collection and to give you a straightforward way to reference your findings. This may be in the form of a simple spreadsheet or checklist that tracks various system functionalities. You may also wish to devise a rubric to score how well each system performs at certain tasks. The approach you take is up to you; it is merely important to keep the information you gather in a format that allows for easy assessment and comparison. This will put you in the best position to make an informed and well-considered decision.

Final Thoughts

While it may seem like a daunting prospect to choose among the plethora of available systems for managing and delivering your digital content to users, the process can help you to better clarify your vision for your digital collections as an end product and to envision how your users will actually interact with them. And with all the time and effort involved in creating your digital collections, you'll want to ensure you're presenting them in the best possible light and providing a positive user experience so that the materials will actually be utilized.

This is where all the pieces come together and the hard work of scanning and metadata creation pays off: when you are able to load your content into a vehicle for it to be displayed and shared with the world. You will likely feel a sense of well-deserved pride after publishing your first collections, the result of creating something that can be at the same time attractive and useful. This can be coupled with the satisfaction of giving new life to materials that may otherwise be little-used or forgotten, since publishing your digitized collections on the Web opens them up to an entirely new audience that would not otherwise be exposed to them. Your materials may even begin to take on a life of their own as they are discovered, shared, commented on, and incorporated into research and scholarship by users from around the world.

REFERENCES

Awre, Chris, and Tom Cramer. 2012. "Building the Hydra Together: Enhancing Repository Provision through Multi-Institution Collaboration." *Journal of Digital Information* 13, no. 1. https://journals.tdl.org/jodi/index.php/jodi/article/view/5879.

Calhoun, Karen. 2014. *Exploring Digital Libraries: Foundations, Practice, Prospects*. London: Facet.

Center for History and New Media (CHNM). 2016. "Omeka:Project." www.omeka.org.

Cervone, H. Frank. 2006. "Some Considerations When Selecting Digital Library Software." *OCLC Systems & Services: International Digital Library Perspectives* 22, no. 3: 107–10. http://doi.org/10.1108/10650750610663987.

Corbett, Hillary, Jimmy Gaphery, Lauren Work, and Sam Byrd. 2016. "Choosing a Repository Platform: Open Source vs. Hosted Solutions." In *Making Institutional Repositories Work*, edited by Burton B. Callicott, David Scherer, and Andrew Wesolek, 3–14. West Lafayette, IN: Purdue University Press.

Crow, Raym. 2002. "The Case for Institutional Repositories: A SPARC Position Paper." Scholarly Publishing and Academic Resources Coalition. www.sparc.arl.org/sites/default/files/ir_final_release_102.pdf.

DeRidder, Jody L. 2007. "Choosing Software for a Digital Library." *Library Hi Tech News* 24, nos. 9/10: 19–21. http://dx.doi.org/10.1108/07419050710874223.

Lagoze, Carl, Sandy Payette, Edwin Shin, and Chris Wilper. 2006. "Fedora: An Architecture for Complex Objects and Their Relationships." *International Journal on Digital Libraries* 6, no. 2: 124–38.

Kucsma, Jason, Kevin Reiss, and Angela Sidman. 2010. "Using Omeka to Build Digital Collections: The METRO Case Study." *D-Lib Magazine* 16, nos. 3/4. doi: 10.1045/march2010-kucsma.

Samuels, Ruth Gallegos, and Henry Griffy. 2012. "Evaluating Open Source Software for Use in Library Initiatives: A Case Study Involving Electronic Publishing." *portal: Libraries and the Academy* 12, no. 1: 41–61. doi: 10.1353/pla.2012.0007.

Smith, MacKenzie, Mary Barton, Mick Bass, et al. 2003. "DSpace: An Open Source Dynamic Digital Repository." *D-Lib Magazine* 9, no. 1. doi: 10.1045/january2003-smith.

Stein, Ayla, and Santi Thompson. 2015. "Taking Control: Identifying Motivations for Migrating Library Digital Asset Management Systems." *D-Lib Magazine* 21, nos. 9/10. doi: 10.1045/september2015-stein.

COPYRIGHT AND DIGITAL COLLECTIONS

WITH THE ADVENT OF DIGITIZATION, TECHNOLOGY HAS made it increasingly easy for the average person to make and share high-quality copies of all types of resources, from texts and images to audio and video. Anyone with a computer and common peripheral equipment such as a scanner or DVD burner can produce nearly unlimited reproductions of an article, photograph, song, or film and distribute it widely online. This capability has driven the explosive growth of digital libraries and now allows even the smallest, resource-challenged cultural heritage institutions to create and disseminate digital content throughout the world. While this provides great benefits in terms of increasing public access to content, the ability to broadly share materials brings with it a heightened need for awareness of the legal rights of content creators and the responsibilities of digital content owners in respecting these rights. The information landscape has changed drastically since the days of paper and ink, and yet intellectual property laws remain largely the same. This can present unique challenges for the digital collections manager and has important implications for the digital collection building process overall.

The roles of cultural heritage institutions have been shaped throughout history in fundamental ways by copyright law, which has in some cases facilitated the very existence of these organizations (throughout this chapter, we will be specifically examining United States copyright law). The ability of libraries to legally lend books and other materials relies on the *first sale doctrine,* which gives the lawful owner of a copyrighted work the right to distribute (resell, rent, or loan) that copy without prior permission from the copyright holder (in other words, the copyright owner is only permitted to control the first sale of the work). The first sale doctrine, which originated with a 1908 Supreme Court ruling and was codified in section 109(a) of U.S. copyright law, functioned well throughout much of the twentieth century. At that time, large-scale reproduction and sharing of copyrighted works was difficult since most were produced in tangible formats such as paper, film, or phonorecord. Furthermore, the creation of physical copies was not required to facilitate the lending or sharing of these works.

Now that much information is produced digitally, the relevance of the first sale doctrine has been eroded. The transfer of tangible works does not easily mirror that of digital works, since first sale does not allow for reproduction and digital distribution generally entails creating an entirely new copy of the work. Subsequently, copyright owners have taken steps to limit the sharing of digital materials through the use of digital rights management (DRM) technologies which are designed to control access and sharing. With the shift to digital, there has also been a movement away from selling content in favor of licensing it, which places limitations on such activities as lending. Licensing tends to remove ownership from the equation, thereby stripping buyers of first sale rights. We can see the effects of this change most readily in libraries with the proliferation of electronic books and journals. Most publishers now license subscriptions to this content, and can in turn place restrictions on how many times an item may circulate to library users as well as the amount of time it may remain in the library's collection before needing to be repurchased. The lack of a "digital first sale" doctrine to govern the sharing of digital works has important implications for libraries and other cultural institutions in the twenty-first century.

The case of the first sale doctrine provides an important illustration of the ways in which the digital revolution has changed the intellectual property landscape for both content creators and consumers, and it also exemplifies how copyright law has struggled to keep pace with this change. There are still many gray areas that remain to be resolved by the courts, and this can result in uncertainty and complications for librarians, archivists, and curators who wish to digitize materials and distribute them online. The aim of this chapter is to provide information necessary for digital content creators and managers to make thoughtful and knowledgeable decisions about what materials they can lawfully digitize and share. This is not always a cut-and-dried process and may involve an element of risk management. While it's not exactly commonplace for a cultural heritage institution to face legal action for copyright infringement, particularly when it comes to the digitization of archival materials, it still pays to know the law and make every effort to maintain compliance with it. To that end, we will start with a brief overview of copyright law and its application to libraries and other cultural institutions.

Copyright Basics

Copyright law in the United States has its basis in the U.S. Constitution. Article 1, Section 8, Clause 8 gives Congress the power "to promote the Progress of Science and useful Arts, by securing for limited Times to Authors and Inventors the exclusive Right to their respective Writings and Discoveries." This clause creates the basis for both U.S. copyright and patent law. Its purpose is to award artists, writers, and scientists with a set of exclusive rights for a limited period of time as a means of encouraging the creation of art and culture and the development of knowledge. The Copyright Act was first implemented in 1790, with the most recent revision occurring in 1976.

The exclusive rights granted to copyright holders include the following:

- The right to reproduce the work;
- The right to create derivatives of the original work;
- The right to distribute copies of the work to the public by sale, lease, or rental; and
- The right to perform and display the work publicly.

By default, the copyright owner is the creator of the work. There are certain exceptions to this rule, including "works for hire." This may be defined as a work prepared by an employee during the course of his or her employment, or a work that is specially ordered or commissioned for use under certain circumstances, such as a contribution to a collective work, a translation, or a compilation. In these cases, copyright is generally held by the employer or commissioning body. In cases of joint authorship, the creators are co-owners of the copyright. In the case of collective works (for example, periodicals) where the creator has not expressly agreed in writing that it is a work for hire, copyright for an individual contribution remains with the creator, and the compiler holds copyright to the collective work as a whole.

Materials that are eligible for copyright protection must be original works that have been fixed in a tangible form of expression, meaning they have been written or otherwise recorded. Facts, data, or other information that does not convey originality on the part of the creator are generally not protected. Works created by employees of the U.S. government as part of their official duties are also typically exempt from copyright protection. Prior to 1976, the route to securing copyright generally required that the work be published with a notice of copyright; however, this is no longer the case. The Copyright Act of 1976 mandated that all works are automatically protected from the moment of their creation. This is an often-misunderstood aspect of copyright law, and many people still assume that a work must be officially published or registered with the U.S. Copyright Office to qualify for protection. An unpublished work, such as a drawing or poem scribbled on a piece of paper or a digital snapshot that is stored on a computer, is protected in equal measure to that of a commercially published book or printed photograph. No action on the part of the creator is required, although it is still possible to register a work or affix a copyright notice to it as a means of formally recording ownership. Copyright registration is in fact advisable, since you can't legally sue for copyright infringement if your work is not registered.

While the main purpose of copyright law is to protect and encourage content creators by awarding them the equivalent of a monopoly over their work, it seeks to balance these individual rights with the rights of the larger public by making the monopoly temporary. The terms of copyright protection have varied over the years, but for works created on or after January 1, 1978 (the date when the Copyright Act of 1976 took effect), copyright generally endures from the moment of creation until 70 years after the author's death. Works for hire, anonymous works, and pseudonymous works have slightly longer terms: 95 years from publication or 120 years from creation, whichever is shorter.

For works that were created prior to January 1, 1978, things get a bit trickier. If a work was created but not published or registered before this date, it is generally subject to the previously described terms imposed by the 1976 Copyright Act. If, however, a work had been created prior to this date and had already secured copyright protection by publication with a copyright notice or registration with the Copyright Office, it fell under the guidelines spelled out in the previous copyright law, the Copyright Act of 1909, which allowed for a term of 28 years with the possibility of subsequent renewal. Due to a number of amendments to the 1976 act, the maximum total term of copyright protection for these works is now 95 years. The above explanation by necessity glosses over many of the intricacies related to how copyright terms are determined for works published prior to 1978, which are unfortunately rather complicated. There are materials available online that can help you sort out the specifics; a good place to start is Peter Hirtle's chart outlining copyright terms for various scenarios (2015).

When the terms of copyright protection for a work expire, then the work enters the *public domain.* Works in the public domain are owned by the public, rather than an individual or organization, so they may be used by anyone without permission. Some materials, including works created by employees of the federal government, enter the public domain at the point of creation because they were never eligible for copyright protection to begin with. In addition, works may be expressly dedicated to the public domain by their creators, in which case the work is essentially donated to the public for unrestricted use. One way of doing this is through the application of a Creative Commons license that allows content creators to opt out of copyright protection. The nonprofit Creative Commons organization (www.creativecommons.org) offers a number of licenses that copyright owners can use to grant various levels of permission that are less restrictive than what default copyright law allows. Works that are marked with a Creative Commons license can generally be considered to be in the public domain under certain circumstances, for example for noncommercial uses or when the creator is attributed. Figure 8.1 shows an example of a Creative Commons license notice denoting the Attribution-NoDerivs license (or CC BY-ND), which allows for redistribution of a work for commercial and noncommercial purposes, as long as the work is unchanged (no derivatives created) and the original creator is attributed. A variety of other types of licenses are available that specify different levels of user permissions.

FIGURE 8.1
Creative Commons CC BY-ND license notice

Determining whether a work has entered the public domain can often be difficult, since it requires keeping track of the various copyright expiration guidelines outlined previously. Furthermore, whether or not a work's copyright has expired can in some cases depend on whether the copyright was renewed within a period stipulated by the law in effect at the time (specifically, works published after 1922 and before 1964 must have been renewed during the twenty-eighth year after publication to avoid entering the public domain). However, there is a point in time before which the expiration terms cease to apply, and that date is January 1, 1923. All works published before this date are automatically in the public domain. It's important to note that this applies only to *published* works; unpublished works created prior to 1923 are subject to protection for the life of the author plus seventy years. According to the Copyright Extension Act of 1998, which effectively placed a twenty-year "freeze" on copyright expiration, no new works will enter the public domain until 2019, when works published in 1923 will expire, followed in 2020 with works published in 1924, and so on.

The information in this section has specifically addressed copyright rules for works that are created in the United States. These guidelines generally also apply to works with foreign origins (those whose authors are not U.S. citizens or nationals, or that were first published abroad). When the United States joined the Berne Convention for the Protection of Literary and Artistic Works in 1989, it agreed to afford protection to works that were still under copyright in their countries of origin (provided the country is also a member of the Berne Convention). The convention has 168 member parties, and between Berne and a number of other international treaties, the United States has reciprocal copyright agreements with most foreign countries. So when determining the duration of copyright for a foreign work, it is generally safe to consider it to be the same as for an American work. However, this does not eliminate the possibility that a work that is in the public domain in the United States is not protected by copyright in another country.

Copyright Exemptions for Cultural Institutions

Another way that U.S. copyright law seeks to balance the rights of copyright owners with those of the general public is by providing for explicit statutory exemptions to the law. These exemptions limit the rights of copyright owners by allowing individuals, in certain situations, to reproduce copyright-protected work without first obtaining permission. The most important exemption is Section 109 of the Copyright Act, or the first sale doctrine, discussed previously. Additionally, Section 108 addresses other exemptions that are explicitly granted to libraries and archives, which allow these institutions to perform the following actions without infringing copyright:

- Make up to three preservation copies of an unpublished work;
- Make up to three replacement copies of a published work that has been damaged, lost, stolen, or is deteriorating or in an obsolete format;
- Make a copy of a work at the request of a patron (excluding certain types of works such as musical and pictorial works and motion pictures);
- Make a copy of a work for interlibrary loan;
- Make a recording of an audiovisual news program;
- Digitize a published work that is in its last twenty years of copyright protection (granted that the work is not currently in print or being licensed and that a copy cannot be obtained at a fair price).

An additional exemption that is not limited exclusively to any particular type of user, but is nonetheless of great importance to cultural heritage institutions, is found in Section 107. Commonly known as the *fair use doctrine,* this statute allows for the reproduction, distribution, or performance of a copyrighted work for purposes such as criticism, comment, news reporting, teaching, scholarship, or research. However, users are not given carte blanche to use any or all of a work under these circumstances. They must make a case that the use is "fair" as determined by the following four factors:

- The purpose and character of the use, including whether such use is of a commercial nature or is for nonprofit educational purposes;
- The nature of the copyrighted work;
- The amount and substantiality of the portion used in relation to the copyrighted work as a whole; and
- The effect of the use upon the potential market for or value of the copyrighted work.

Each of the four factors must be analyzed in terms of whether or not they favor fair use. In general, uses that are educational or nonprofit in purpose or that have a "transformative" effect are more likely to be fair than commercial uses, while use of factual and scholarly works is typically considered more fair than that of creative or original works. Using the smallest possible amount of a work generally weighs in favor of fair use, while using the "heart," or most important part of the work, weighs against it. If a version of the work is available for purchase, use is less likely to be fair than if the work is unavailable by traditional means (for example, if it is out of print). The four factors must be considered in relation to each other and according to the specifics of the situation. Therefore, there is no universal approach to applying fair use, and each case must be treated individually. This open-endedness makes the fair use exemption highly flexible, but can also make it confusing and difficult to apply. However, taking the time to construct a fair use argument can be worth the effort. According to Section 504(c)(3) of the Copyright Act, a nonprofit educational institution, library, or archive that has reasonable grounds to believe their use of a work is fair use may not be subject to statutory damages for infringement.

Finally, the doctrine of *sovereign immunity* is not technically a copyright exemption, but in some cases it may be used as an argument to protect against damages associated with copyright infringement. According to the Eleventh Amendment, state and tribal governments, and by extension component entities such as state universities, cannot be sued in federal court for damages related to intellectual property infringement. However, copyright owners may still sue state agencies for injunctive relief (request that the court make the agency discontinue use of the infringing material), and there also remains the possibility that an individual state employee may be sued for monetary damages. In 1990 Congress passed an amendment to the Copyright Act (the Copyright Remedy Clarification Act) that attempted to nullify states' immunity from copyright violation suits, but the act has been struck down as unconstitutional by various courts and has not been enforced against a state to date.

Orphan Works

At this point, you may be noticing a trend: complying with copyright law can be complicated, cumbersome, and confusing. But there is one more layer of complexity that can be particularly problematic for libraries and other institutions wishing to create digital collections. This issue arose as a result of the Copyright Act of 1976, which eliminated the requirement that works must be registered in order to obtain copyright protection. Consequently, no centralized recording system has been maintained to track and identify copyright holders. This situation has created an entire class of *orphan works* that exist in a state of copyright limbo.

In addition to making use of the exceptions contained in Sections 107, 108, and 109, if one wishes to reproduce a work that is under copyright, a straightforward way of attempting this is to contact the copyright holder and request their permission. In certain circumstances, especially in the case of older works that no longer command much, if any, market value, the rights holder may be willing to simply grant permission for its use (this permission should always be secured in writing). For published works, locating and contacting the copyright holder, whether it is an organization or individual, is generally a fairly straightforward process—if the creator or publisher's information is not clearly marked on the work itself, often a quick Internet search will be sufficient to track it down. But what if the copyright holder is impossible to identify, or the person is known but cannot be located? This is a particular concern for unpublished works. Additionally, in the case of older works, the copyright may have changed hands over the years and records tracing this exchange may be lost, or the organization that originally published the work may no longer exist. Works of this status are considered orphans, and their use may be an infringement of copyright.

Orphan works present something of a catch-22 for users. While it may be entirely possible that a copyright holder would grant permission to use a work if asked, the fact that the person or organization cannot be identified means that, outside of what is permitted for exemptions such as fair use, the work is de facto off limits to users until such time as it has entered the public domain. And under a system where copyright terms are calculated according to the life span of the creator, if the identity of the rights holder is unknown, the date that copyright expires on the work may be difficult or impossible to determine. The quandary for users is that they may have every intention of following the letter of the law, but are hindered from doing so by an inability to obtain the necessary information. Use of an orphan work places them at risk of being sued for infringement should the rights holder emerge at a future time.

The U.S. Copyright Office recognizes the problem that orphan works present, stating on its website that "the Office has long shared the concern with many in the copyright community that the uncertainty surrounding the ownership status of orphan works does not serve the objectives of the copyright system. For good faith users, orphan works are a frustration, a liability risk, and a major cause of gridlock in the digital marketplace" (United States Copyright Office 2015a). The office has issued reports that address the problem of orphan works in general (United States Copyright Office 2006) and as it relates to the practice of mass digitization (United States Copyright Office 2015b). Legislative bills were introduced in Congress in 2006 and 2008 that proposed solutions to the problem, including protections for nonprofit organizations such as libraries and creation of a database of visual works, but neither one ultimately passed. For now, users are left to shoulder the burden of tracking down elusive copyright holders, and to weigh the risks inherent in the use of orphan works.

Identifying and Locating Copyright Owners

In most cases, if you wish to locate a copyright holder with the goal of requesting permission to reproduce his or her work, you are going to have to do some detective work—both to determine who the rights holder is, and how they may be contacted. In the best-case scenario, copyright information is clearly printed on the work and the information is current and easy to follow up on. But it isn't unusual that you may run into one or more of the following stumbling blocks: the work is unmarked, the copyright has changed hands or been transferred over the years, the publisher is now defunct, or little to no information is publicly available about the creator. These obstacles can be difficult, but not impossible, to overcome, and there are tools available that can make the task of identification easier.

If you are investigating the ownership status of a published work, it's a good idea to start at the source: the U.S. Copyright Office. The Copyright Office maintains an online records catalog containing copyright registrations and renewals for all post-1978 works. For works prior to 1978, the Copyright Office has digitized the physical volumes of the Catalog of Copyright Entries and made them available to the public through the Internet Archive (discussed in chapter 4). Both the online catalog and the virtual catalogs can be accessed via the U.S. Copyright Office website at www.copyright.gov/records. Keep in mind that these sources may not reflect whether copyright has been transferred from the original owner, as it is not required that this data be recorded.

Another online tool that may be useful for identifying a copyright owner is the WATCH File, www.watch-file.com. WATCH stands for "Writers, Artists, and Their Copyright Holders," and this database tracks information about the works of prominent authors, artists, and people in other creative fields. For a given work, the database can provide information about the current copyright holder or the holder's representative. An outgrowth of the WATCH File is the FOB (Firms Out of Business) File, www.fob-file.com. This database provides information about printers, publishers, and literary agencies that are now defunct, and indicates when possible if there is a successor organization that may currently own any surviving rights.

If the aforementioned resources fail to bear fruit, you may wish to consult what are known as collective licensing agencies or reproduction rights organizations. These organizations, which may charge a fee for their services, typically exist for individual industries and provide centralized copyright ownership information. They may also act as agents for copyright holders and negotiate permissions on their behalf. Examples of these organizations include the following:

- For works in print, the Copyright Clearance Center (www.copyright.com) and the Authors Registry (www.authorsregistry.org); and
- For works of visual art, the Artists Rights Society (www.arsny.com) and the Visual Artists and Galleries Association (http://vagarights.com).

For musical works, there are two levels of copyright protection, one for the song itself (for example, the musical notation and lyrics written on the sheet music) and another for any recordings of the song. For permission to reproduce written music, you will need to contact the music publisher directly, or use a performing rights organization such as the American Society of Composers, Authors, and Publishers (www.ascap.com); Broadcast Music, Inc. (www.bmi.com); or the Society of European Stage Authors and Composers (www.sesac.com). For rights to a specific recording of a song, you will generally need to contact the record company in addition to the music publisher. Keep in mind that while a piece of music may be in the public domain, a particular recording of it may be under copyright.

If you are dealing with unpublished works such as manuscripts, photographs, or ephemera, chances are they may be part of an archival or special collection at your institution, so you will want to start by examining any available records such as a deed of gift to determine who the copyright owner is. In some cases, the creator may have sold or transferred copyright to your institution when the collection was donated or purchased. If acquisition documentation does not prove helpful, check to see if related materials in the collection can provide any hints; examining the collection finding aid might also yield fruitful connections. In the case of an academic institution, an alumni or donor relations office may have retained contact information for individuals who hold copyright for certain materials. Most institutional records would likely be considered works for hire and belong to the institution itself.

When all else fails, your best strategy may be to harness the power of the Internet to cull as much information as possible about the work and its creator. This type of sleuthing can yield some valuable clues about copyright ownership, but the material you find may not be complete or authoritative enough to allow you to come to a definitive conclusion. You will likely have to be fairly creative and tenacious, and be willing to follow up on any information that arises. This may include posting queries to forums or e-mail lists, and doing genealogical research to track down family members or heirs of the creator in order to determine current ownership. Realistically, some of these searches will end up failing, in which case it would be reasonable to consider the item an orphan work.

The Society of American Archivists has put together a useful report outlining best practices for dealing with orphan works (SAA 2009). Not only does it outline strategies for identifying and locating copyright owners, it also offers advice regarding how much effort should be made for different types of works. You can easily spend countless hours conducting a copyright investigation for a given work, and common sense suggests that this is not always an efficient use of time or money for small and underfunded organizations. The report suggests that searches involving more recent works have a higher likelihood of success, as do those for professional authors and artists. Your decision to engage in a minimal or extensive search should be informed by these characteristics, as well as risk factors that will be addressed later in the chapter. Either way, it's advisable to keep a record of all attempts made to locate a copyright owner, even if the investigation is unsuccessful.

Requesting and Securing Permissions

If you are successful in identifying and locating a copyright owner, before you set about contacting that person or organization you will want to determine the types of rights that you would like to request. Are you seeking exclusive or nonexclusive rights? It is unlikely that you would seek exclusive rights, as this limits the copyright owner's ability to grant permission to others to use the work as well. You will also want to decide what terms of use you wish to seek, or what length of time you would like to use the work, for example one-time use or use in perpetuity. Finally, think about whether you are willing to pay a fee to the copyright owner for permission, and if so, how much that amount would be.

If you have determined that copyright is owned by an existing publisher, you may find that the company provides a permission agreement form on their website that you may download and fill out. In many cases, however, you will need to compose your own written request to be delivered via mail, e-mail, or fax. Your correspondence should contain detailed information concerning your request, including:

- Who you are
- What the work is you would like to use and how much
- What the nature of your use is (e.g., noncommercial/educational)
- Where the work will be used (e.g., public website)
- How long you plan to use the work (e.g., indefinitely)

The more specific your request, the more effective it is likely to be. A copyright holder may be unlikely to respond to a request or grant permission if it is not clear to them what you are asking for.

If the copyright owner does grant your request, be sure to get the permission in writing, preferably with a signature. Keep copies of all correspondence and forms in a file for your records. It is wise to keep a record of all attempts made to identify and contact a copyright owner, whether they are successful or not—in the event that there is a challenge to your use of the work, you will have evidence of your good faith efforts to comply with the law. This is especially true for orphan works, as you may decide to move forward with your use despite being unable to identify or locate the copyright owner, having concluded from your investigation that the use will likely go unchallenged. Weighing such a decision and documenting your search for information are elements of risk management that may come into play when engaging in collection development for digital collections.

Managing Risk

Libraries and other cultural institutions have always had to maintain a certain level of awareness of copyright law, as it has a direct effect on many activities that these organizations undertake. Indeed, as Jeffrey Graveline points out, librarians are often seen as the copyright police, since they are on the "front lines of access to information" and are often in a position to tell others what they can and cannot do (2010). But with the advent of digital reproduction and the shift to widespread online information access, even seasoned and knowledgeable information professionals can be left feeling unsure about how to comply with copyright law while building digital collections. Digitization has in many ways muddied the copyright waters, and even the law itself has lagged to some extent in addressing this upheaval. Facing such uncertainties, some in the cultural heritage community—particularly those at smaller institutions—may be hesitant to make their materials available to the wider community online, fearing that the risk incurred is too great.

While it is undoubtedly wise to proceed cautiously, copyright fears should not lead to the total avoidance of digitization projects. Rather, a clear understanding of the risks should guide you in your approach to collection development on a project-by-project basis. Copyright should be taken into account from the beginning stages of project planning, and strategies developed to address and minimize risk. At the same time, approaches to copyright cannot be generalized across institutions. Each institution must assess its own level of risk tolerance and proceed accordingly. For example, mass digitization projects such as those undertaken by Google to digitize millions of books in partnership with large research libraries from around the world carry with them a rather high level of risk. As we saw in chapter 4, in the case of the Google Books project, the Authors Guild did bring a lawsuit against Google in 2005 to halt the scanning of in-copyright books—although in a series of rulings in the decade since then, the courts have decided in favor of Google (citing fair use, in light of the fact that only "snippets" of these works were made available online). In this situation, well-funded institutions such as Harvard University and the University of Oxford were willing to place themselves at considerable risk by partnering with Google for what they believed to be a good cause, and the resources available to these organizations in the event of a lawsuit would have carried much weight in this decision (not to mention the support of a billion-dollar company like Google). Obviously, most institutions would not be in the position to take on such risk.

In determining the level of risk which your organization is comfortable with, you must weigh a number of factors. Hirtle, Hudson, and Kenyon (2009) refer to this process as "risk analysis calculus," and lay out a number of questions that should be addressed, including:

- What factors increase the risk my institution faces?
- How likely is it that I might be sued?
- What are the potential damages?
- What strategies can my institution follow to minimize risk?

Factors that increase risk include orphan work status, uncertainty as to whether a work is in the public domain (either in the United States or another country), and the possibility that there is more than one copyright attached to a single work, as may be the case with a musical recording. Factors contributing to the likelihood of legal action may include whether the work still has any market value, whether the copyright holder is still alive, and whether the copyright holder would likely have the means to mount a lawsuit (less likely for an individual than a corporation). It is worth noting that court cases involving copyright infringement by libraries, archives, and museums are rare, and so estimating potential damages can be difficult. High-profile cases of copyright litigation have been known to result in hundreds of thousands and even millions of dollars in damages and attorney fees. But for many copyright holders, the high cost of litigation is not worth the low return that would likely result from action against a cultural heritage institution that may be protected against an award of damages by an argument of sovereign immunity or fair use. Finally, it is likely that the first step taken by a copyright owner would be to issue a cease and desist notice (often called a "takedown notice") or request for payment rather than immediately filing a lawsuit, allowing the institution to take preventive action to avoid legal proceedings.

After weighing these factors, there are a variety of strategies that an individual institution may decide to use to manage the risks of digitization. For the most risk-averse, these include limiting digitization activities strictly to works in which copyright is owned by the institution, works that are clearly in the public domain, or works for which written permission has been secured by the copyright owner. A more risk-tolerant approach may allow for the digitization of orphan works following an investigation and documented efforts to identify or contact the copyright owner, along with a notice that the items will be removed should the owner come forward to make such a request. The decision may also be made to digitize works that are known to be copyright-protected, given that a strong fair use argument can be made (this argument should be documented and retained in the event the use is challenged). Keep in mind that it is difficult to use a fair use argument to justify digitizing and distributing an entire copyrighted work, so fair use may be of limited usefulness for many digitization projects.

Whatever your justification may be for digitizing and distributing a given work, it is generally a good idea to provide an explanation on your website as to the nature of your use. This may be as simple as including a rights statement in the metadata record indicating that copyright is owned by your institution or that you believe the work to be in the public domain. If you have secured permission from the copyright holder, be sure to clearly state this and cite them as such. In the case of orphan works, it may be a good idea to invite potential copyright holders or others with information about the copyright to contact you. In addition to protecting your institution, providing information about copyright status also assists your patrons in determining what use they are lawfully permitted to make of a digitized work.

Final Thoughts

It is nearly impossible to completely avoid risk when it comes to copyright and digitization—ultimately, there is no guarantee that your use of a work won't be challenged, even if it is completely legal. But as this chapter aims to demonstrate, cultural heritage professionals need not live in fear of such occurrences. The law provides for a balance between the rights of copyright holders and those of cultural institutions and the public in general. The challenge for librarians, archivists, and curators is striking the right balance, one that combines respect for copyright holders with a desire to uphold "their missions of preserving and facilitating access to intellectual and creative works" (Hirtle, Hudson, and Kenyon 2009). All it takes is the basic knowledge to make reasoned, thoughtful decisions.

To that end, this chapter has provided a broad overview to get you started. But copyright is a complex topic that cannot be adequately summarized in a single chapter. In order to better understand the nuances of the law and make truly informed decisions, it is recommended that you take the time to delve a bit deeper into copyright issues as they relate to cultural heritage institutions. There are plenty of good books available to further illuminate the subject, including those by Russell (2004), Crews (2012), and Gathegi (2012). Armed with this information, you can confidently move forward with your digitization projects knowing that you are protecting yourself and your institution to the greatest extent possible.

REFERENCES

Crews, Kenneth D. 2012. *Copyright Law for Librarians and Educators: Creative Strategies and Practical Strategies.* 3rd edition. Chicago: American Library Association.

Gathegi, John N. 2012. *The Digital Librarian's Legal Handbook.* New York: Neal-Schuman.

Graveline, Jeffrey D. 2010. "Debunking Common Misconceptions and Myths." *College and Undergraduate Libraries* 17, no. 1: 100–105. doi: 10.1080/10691310903584650.

Hirtle, Peter. 2015. "Copyright Term and the Public Domain in the United States, 1 January 2015." Cornell University Copyright Information Center. https://copyright.cornell.edu/resources/publicdomain.cfm.

Hirtle, Peter, Emily Hudson, and Andrew T. Kenyon. 2009. *Copyright and Cultural Institutions: Guidelines for Digitization for U.S. Libraries, Archives, and Museums.* Ithaca, NY: Cornell University Library.

Russell, Carrie. 2004. *Complete Copyright: An Everyday Guide for Librarians.* Chicago: American Library Association.

Society of American Archivists (SAA). 2009. "Orphan Works: Statement of Best Practices." http://www2.archivists.org/sites/all/files/OrphanWorks-June2009.pdf.

United States Copyright Office. 2015a. http://copyright.gov/orphan.

———. 2015b. "Orphan Works and Mass Digitization." http://copyright.gov/orphan/reports/orphan-works2015.pdf.

———. 2006. "Report on Orphan Works." http://copyright.gov/orphan/orphan-report-full.pdf.

PRESERVING YOUR DIGITAL ASSETS

AT THIS POINT YOU'VE GOTTEN A GENERAL OVERVIEW OF the various steps involved in creating a digital collection, from physical material selection and reformatting to description and online delivery. Once you have your digital content loaded into a DCMS or other software platform for patrons to use, it may be tempting to consider your job done. However, this is not the case. Just as physical objects in a library, museum, or archive require continued attention in the form of conservation and preservation measures if they are to remain usable over the years, so too do digital objects. In fact, the threat of deterioration for digital materials is in many ways more pressing than it is for analog materials, and the preservation of digital content can be more complex. For this reason, the final step in the digital collections process, that of preserving your digital assets, is in many ways the most important. There could be no worse outcome for the librarian, archivist, or curator than to spend countless hours reformatting and describing digital files, only to have them rendered inaccessible or obsolete at a future time. To avoid this fate, it is important to familiarize yourself with the theoretical and practical aspects of digital preservation.

The advent of personal computers and the Internet has sparked a huge increase in the production of digital content over the past few decades, from electronic documents, images, audio, and video to web pages and research data. While this tidal wave of data provides great value in the form of increased accessibility to information, there is growing concern that the intellectual and cultural artifacts of our time are at risk of being lost due to the fragility and ephemerality of digital formats. Some have warned of the coming of a "digital dark age," in which the historic record will be rendered virtually unavailable due to a failure to properly preserve the digital media on which this information is currently being stored. Some have cautioned that this situation has already come to pass, including Terry Kuny, who stated as far back as 1997 that "enormous amounts of digital information are already lost forever" (Kuny 1997).

Think about the digital photos you have taken over the last few years. Unlike the photo album or shoebox of snapshots from years past, which may sit in a closet for decades with little harm to the objects housed inside, these digital images are inherently unstable. Do you take purposeful measures to ensure that they will remain viewable ten, twenty, or fifty years from now? If you're like the majority of people, the answer is no, and you have probably given the matter little thought. You may have these files stored on a device, like a computer or smartphone, but what happens when that device breaks or becomes obsolete, as it inevitably will? Or you may have your images stored on social media or another online platform, such as Flickr or Facebook, thinking that the cloud is a safe place. But what happens if the company that maintains this platform goes out of business? While predictions of a "digital dark age" may seem alarmist, when you really stop to consider it, the threat is real. On a personal scale it may mean only the loss of a few family photos or home videos (which may in itself be a minor tragedy), but on a larger scale the repercussions for the historical record could be severe.

For cultural heritage institutions charged with upholding our history for future generations, the issue of digital preservation looms large. Libraries, archives, and museums that create or maintain digital collections must make an active, sustained, and concerted effort at the institutional level to ensure the long-term accessibility and readability of their digital assets. This may seem like a daunting prospect, particularly for smaller organizations that lack technical resources and expertise. But while the field of digital preservation is still relatively new, there are best practices that have emerged which any organization can incorporate into their digitization program. These will be outlined in the following pages, but first, it's important to understand why digital data is so vulnerable to loss and decay. This knowledge will be crucial as you begin to strategize a digital preservation plan for your own institution.

Dangers to Digital Data

Anyone who's handled an old book or manuscript can easily see the effects that time can have on a physical document. Over the years, paper fades, becomes discolored, and eventually falls apart without proper preservation action being taken to prevent this outcome. Generally, this decay will occur over decades or centuries, depending on the document's storage conditions. More stable media, such as clay or stone tablets, can remain intact and legible for millennia, if not indefinitely.

In contrast, digital media are uniquely fragile and vulnerable to decay, and this deterioration can be invisible to the naked eye. You can't necessarily look at a digital storage device and determine whether any of the files contained within it have been damaged. Yet, damage to digital objects is an all-too-common occurrence, which can happen more or less spontaneously and without warning. You may have had the experience of trying to access a digital file that you thought was safely saved to a CD, DVD, or USB flash drive, only to find that the file would not open—it had been corrupted. Or perhaps you've had a computer hard drive unexpectedly crash, erasing all your data. These situations reflect one of the major dangers to digital data, which is *media degradation*. Digital media are highly susceptible to physical decay that can cause data loss, which is often referred to as *bit rot* (so-called because digital objects are made up of bitstreams of ones and zeroes, and the proper functioning of these objects depends on the integrity of the bitstreams being maintained). Data loss can be attributed to many factors, including physical scratches on the surface of the storage medium, demagnetization, warping caused by excessive humidity or temperature variation, or errors in the data-recording process.

Media degradation is also the inevitable result of the passage of time. Compared with physical materials such as paper or photographic negatives, digital media have a surprisingly short life span. There are three basic types of digital storage media: magnetic (including magnetic tape, floppy disks, and hard-disk drives), solid-state (primarily flash memory), and optical (CDs, DVDs, and Blu-ray discs). These media can generally be expected to degrade in a matter of years or decades. Hard-disk drives may have a data life expectancy as low as one to seven years, while flash drives and solid-state drives fare slightly better at ten to twelve years (Lunt 2011). Optical discs are generally considered to be the best storage option in terms of longevity, but even this format has a limited life span. In a study of optical storage media, the Library of Congress in partnership with the National Institute of Standards and Technology tested the durability of recordable CDs and DVDs and found that their life expectancies ranged from less than fifteen years to more than forty-five years (LC/NIST 2007). In archival terms, where materials are expected to be stored and made accessible in perpetuity, this is a fairly short amount of time.

In addition to media degradation, *technological obsolescence* is another major factor in the loss of digital data—in fact, it is often an even greater threat. Technological obsolescence refers to the process whereby hardware and software become superseded by newer versions, rendering the older versions incompatible with current technology. With time, newer technologies become standard and older formats fall out of use, so that it becomes increasingly difficult to access digital data that depends on the older formats for translation. This is most likely a phenomenon that you have experienced in your everyday life. Do you have any old 3½" or 5¼" floppy disks in your closet from the 1980s or 1990s, and if so do you currently own a computer with a disk drive that can read them? In all likelihood you will not have maintained a functioning machine that is capable of accessing the files on these disks, so for all intents and purposes their contents are unavailable to you, even though the disks themselves may remain physically undamaged.

There are myriad similar examples of "dead" technologies that have fallen by the wayside over the years, for example Beta video equipment, 16-mm home movie projectors, and more recently, VHS tapes. The problem of software obsolescence is somewhat newer, but no less serious. For example, if you were to find a 1990s-era computer with a floppy disk drive that could read one of the old disks in your closet, you would then be presented with the problem of finding a functioning version of a software program that could interpret the files contained on the disks. Your disks may contain text documents that were created with now-defunct or hard-to-find word processing programs like WordStar or AppleWorks, and if those programs are not installed on your 1990s-era computer, you will be hard-pressed to find copies for purchase on the modern market.

Today, technology development moves forward at an astonishing pace, with manufacturers announcing new releases of computers, tablets, smartphones, processors, storage devices, and software on a daily basis. The challenge presented by this rapid proliferation of new media formats is especially significant for librarians, archivists, and curators working with unique born-digital content. As more and more materials are being created and maintained in an exclusively digital format, it is increasingly important that data stewards monitor new technology developments so that this data does not eventually become irrecoverable, lost amid the progression of evolving storage media and software.

What Is Digital Preservation?

The problems outlined above add an extra layer of complexity to the digital collection building process. They reflect the fact that the life of a digital object does not end once it has been created, described, and made available to users. In many ways, these actions mark merely the beginning of the digital object life cycle. Active management of digital assets is required if they are to remain accessible and usable over the long term. This is where the practice of digital preservation comes into play, and although it is a crucial step, it is one that can be easily overlooked in the digitization planning process.

As mentioned in chapter 1, digital preservation is not the same thing as digitization for preservation, the act of creating a digital surrogate of an item for the purpose of preserving the physical original. Digital preservation refers specifically to methods applied to digital content in order to safeguard its integrity over time. According to the Association for Library Collections and Technical Services,

> Digital preservation combines policies, strategies and actions to ensure access to reformatted and born digital content regardless of the challenges of media failure and technological change. The goal of digital preservation is the accurate rendering of authenticated content over time. (ALCTS Preservation and Reformatting Section 2007)

156 \ PART II: BASIC SKILLS

This definition reflects the broad scope of the concept of digital preservation and the fact that it involves multiple activities, from the wide-ranging (policy development) to the specific (performance of explicit procedures).

An important aspect of digital preservation is that it is a deliberate, formal endeavor. While traditional print objects may be left untouched for decades and remain relatively stable, digital objects require active management throughout their life spans if they are to remain viable. Therefore, it is important to incorporate digital preservation planning into the early stages of the digitization process. Preservation should be taken into consideration from the point of creation of the digital object, and ideally even earlier in the form of well-articulated institutional policies and guidelines.

To be effective, digital preservation requires a clear commitment at the institutional level that seeks to balance financial, human, and technological resources. In this vein, the "three-legged stool" model is often used as a metaphor for the framework required for a successful digital preservation program. This concept was developed as part of the Digital Preservation Management Workshop series at Cornell University (which produced a very useful online tutorial addressing digital preservation basics that can be found at www.pworkshop.org.dpm-eng/eng_index.html). Taken together, the three legs of the stool—organizational infrastructure, technological infrastructure, and resources framework—are the core components that serve to balance an institution's overall digital preservation program. The organizational leg encompasses such programmatic elements as policies, procedures, objectives, and staffing. The technological leg consists of such components as hardware, software, and other tools that are used to implement an institution's digital preservation objectives. The resources leg includes initial and ongoing funding required to develop and maintain the digital preservation program. Figure 9.1 presents a visual depiction of the three-legged stool.

FIGURE 9.1
Three-legged stool for digital preservation

Source: Cornell University Library, Digital Preservation Management Workshop (2003).

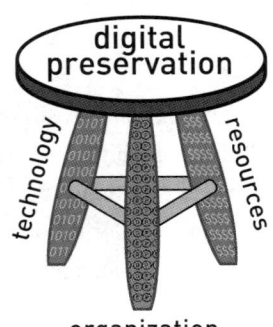

It's important to understand what digital preservation entails at a broad level, but that still leaves the question: how exactly do you *do* digital preservation? There are several practical strategies that you can employ, and the cultural heritage community has developed various best practices for dealing with the problems of media degradation and technological obsolescence. The following section outlines some common techniques for safeguarding digital data over the long term.

Digital Preservation Strategies

The most basic-level digital preservation strategy is one that you are probably already familiar with and have implemented when dealing with important work-related or personal data. *Bitstream copying,* so-called because it involves creating an exact bit-by-bit duplicate of a digital object, is the simple act of backing up your data. It may also be referred to as *replication* or *data redundancy.* Best practice dictates that duplicates should be stored in both local systems and geographically remote systems, so as to minimize the risk that a disastrous event could eliminate both the original and copy. While bitstream copying is important in that it forms the foundation for all other preservation strategies, it is not in itself a sufficient technique for long-term maintenance and should be combined with the other strategies outlined below.

Similarly, *refreshing* involves the bit-level copying of a digital object, but in this case the data is transferred between two types of the same long-term storage medium. For example, you might transfer data from an old, decaying tape or scratched CD to a new tape or CD. Refreshing can address the problems of media degradation and technological obsolescence related to storage media, and should be performed periodically depending on the expected life span of the particular storage format being used.

Refreshing is often considered to be a form of the broader preservation practice known as *migration.* Migration entails the conversion of a digital object from a technology that is at risk of becoming obsolete to a more current technology. This strategy may apply to hardware, in which an object is copied from an older generation of hardware to a newer one, or software, in which an object is transferred from one file format or software program to another. In contrast with bitstream copying and refreshing, migration transforms the digital object itself, which means that it may lose some information in the process (for instance, in the case of a text document, some of the original formatting may be eliminated in the change from one file format to another). The purpose of migration is to preserve the basic intellectual content of the original data while ensuring that it remains fully accessible and functional to users. Migration is one of the most widely practiced digital preservation strategies, but it can be expensive and time-consuming, and repeated migrations can result in significant data loss over time. Migration tends to be most effective for simple digital materials rather than complex ones, such as multimedia objects.

Migration focuses on the content of the digital object itself, in contrast with another primary preservation method, *emulation,* which focuses instead on the hardware and software environment in which the object was originally created. Emulation seeks to retain the look and feel of a digital object by re-creating the experience of using the original. This is done through the development of "software that mimics obsolete systems on current and future generations of computers by emulating applications, operating systems, and/or (most commonly) hardware architecture" (Harvey 2010). A common use for emulators today is to run old computer games on modern computers. However, an example of emulation as a digital preservation method employed by a cultural heritage institution can be found at Emory University's Salman Rushdie Digital Archives Project, where the author's computer files can be accessed via a simulation of the original computing environment of his donated 1990s-era Macintosh computer (Emory University's Stuart A. Rose Manuscript, Archives, and Rare Book Library, n.d.). Since the method of emulation requires the creation of an emulator program, there may be a large commitment of technical and human resources involved. Widespread use of emulation in the future would likely rely on the creation of consortia to develop and make available emulators for smaller institutions that lack these resources.

Closely related to emulation is the process of *encapsulation.* Encapsulation entails the grouping or "packaging" together of a digital object in its original form as a bitstream, along with whatever information may be necessary to maintain access to it in the future. This information may include metadata, software viewers, or software specifications for emulation. The idea behind encapsulation is to maintain together as a unit all the critical components for decoding and rendering an object, to make the object self-describing and minimize the likelihood that any individual component will be lost. This grouping is achieved by using a "wrapper" or "container" such as an XML document. The concept of encapsulation is important to understand because it factors into the Open Archival Information System (OAIS) Reference Model, a widely used international standard in the cultural heritage community that provides a conceptual framework for the design and implementation of digital archival systems. The OAIS information model is based on the concept of an "information package," which is an encapsulated data object that contains the digital object itself along with metadata and "packaging" information that binds the components together. (An entire chapter could easily be devoted to OAIS; for a more thorough guide to the model, see Lavoie 2014). In their digital preservation efforts, many major institutions seek to become OAIS-compliant, meaning that they commit to developing a repository that complies with the OAIS standard. While it is unlikely that a small institution will undertake this process, you may encounter the OAIS model if you decide to transfer your digital information to an OAIS-compliant repository for preservation, in which case it would need to be submitted as an encapsulated information package.

When data is transferred between repositories as in the scenario above, there is increased risk for a digital file to be corrupted or changed. Over time, bit rot can also cause digital objects in long-term storage media to decay. Ensuring that digital objects retain their integrity and authenticity in situations such as these is one of the major goals of digital preservation. But how do you know if your digital material has been damaged or altered at the bit level? This is where *fixity checking* comes into play. "Fixity" refers to "the property of a digital file or object being fixed or unchanged . . . and is synonymous with bit-level integrity" (NDSA 2014). Fixity checking is a means of verifying that digital content has remained stable over time, and is commonly performed through the use of *checksums.* The checksum can be thought of as a digital fingerprint; it is a unique sequence of letters and numbers, generated by a computer algorithm, which represents the bitstream of an individual file. This sequence will change if the file is altered at the bit level, so fixity is verified by comparing the original checksum to one that is newly generated. Fixity checking may be performed at the time that files are transferred or ingested into a repository, and again at regular intervals. Various programs are available for executing fixity checking, and some DCMS and archival storage systems have fixity checking built in. Assuming you are maintaining multiple copies of each digital object, if a corruption is detected then the affected file can simply be replaced.

A final technique worth noting is *normalization,* which essentially refers to the standardization of data formats. Normalization can be considered a form of migration in which digital objects of a specific type, for example image or text files, are converted into a single, more preservation-friendly file format. The target file format is one that has been determined to be more viable over the long term; it will typically be an open rather than proprietary format that is widely used by other established repositories. An illustration of normalization in action would be the decision by an institution to convert all text files that are received in a commercially licensed software format, such as Microsoft Office, into an open format such as PDF/Archival (PDF/A) or Open Document Format (ODF) prior to ingesting them into a digital repository or archival storage system. Normalization addresses the issue of file format obsolescence, and serves to simplify other digital preservation strategies such as migration by limiting the number of file formats involved.

Preservation Metadata

Digital preservation is not a one-size-fits-all endeavor. Some of the strategies outlined in the previous section will be more practical or appropriate for a given institution to implement than others, depending on the institution's size and resources. But regardless of the methods employed, there is one common aspect that is crucial for effective digital preservation: metadata. The successful preservation of digital objects depends in large part on the descriptive and technical information that accompanies them, and the preservation strategies outlined above are highly dependent on good metadata in order to be useful. A lack of metadata can pose serious challenges for digital preservation, for reasons similar to those given in chapter 6 regarding why metadata is important for other aspects of digital collection creation and management. As Lavoie and Gartner state, metadata establishes an "informational frame of reference" around a digital object that is carried with it over time, and "the ability to exploit the full value of a preserved digital object into the future requires preserving this frame of reference in the form of well-maintained preservation metadata" (Lavoie and Gartner 2013).

"Preservation metadata" is not, strictly speaking, itself a separate category of metadata. Rather, it is an amalgamation of the metadata types outlined in chapter 6 (descriptive, administrative, and structural). Metadata from each of these three types contributes value to the preservation process. Just as a digital object placed in a DCMS requires metadata in order to be discoverable and accessible, so too do files placed in long-term storage of any kind. On a basic level, no digital preservation strategy can effectively be applied to a digital object if it cannot first be identified and located via descriptive metadata. Structural metadata describing the relationships between components of a complex digital object is necessary for reconstructing the object and maintaining its integrity over time. Administrative metadata is critical for preserving a record of the digital object's provenance and the context in which it was created, and for providing data that will verify the authenticity and integrity of the object. These types of metadata can include information about the chain of custody and any previous preservation actions that may have been applied to the materials.

The category of administrative metadata also includes a subset, technical metadata, which is of particular importance for preservation. Technical metadata describes the technical attributes of digital objects that will enable their future reproduction and use. Examples of technical metadata include file format, size, and resolution; information about hardware, software, and operating systems that were used to create the object; and fixity information. The types of technical metadata included will be specific to the media format of the digital object. For a still image you will likely want to record information such as dimensions and bit depth, whereas for a digital audio file you may instead include the sample rate. Most technical metadata can be captured and recorded automatically by the equipment that is used to create the digital object, such as a digital camera, scanner, or audio recorder, at the point of data creation.

Another subset of administrative metadata that has significance for purposes of digital preservation is rights management metadata. Since preserving a digital object involves making multiple copies and sometimes modifying the original, copyright or intellectual property limitations may have an effect on a repository's ability to preserve a digital object or provide access to it. It is therefore crucial that information about the legal ownership of a digital object be preserved, along with any access conditions that may have been agreed upon with the original depositor or rights holder. Without this information, it may be difficult or impossible to effectively preserve the materials or legally give users access to them.

Finally, no overview of preservation metadata would be complete without mention of *persistent identifiers,* or PIDS, which contribute to the accessibility and long-term use of digital objects. A PID is a standardized method of identification, a unique sequence of alphanumeric characters that is assigned to an object and remains with it even if its location changes (for example, if it is moved to a different server or repository); it can also help differentiate between several different versions of an object. A PID can be likened to a social security number in that it is permanently associated with the object throughout its life span and is independent of name or address changes. Various standard frameworks exist that support the creation and management of PIDs for digital objects on the Web. These include the Uniform Resource Name (URN), the Persistent Uniform Resource Locator (PURL), the Digital Object Locator (DOI), and the Archival Resource Key (ARK). Much more can be said about the topic of PIDs and how they function; a good overview of current standards and their application has been written by Emma Tonkin (2008).

Preservation Metadata Standards

Priscilla Caplan writes, "Preservation metadata represents a repository's best guess as to what information will be necessary in order to make it possible to use a digital item in the future, given the likelihood of changes in technology, format obsolescence, and other risks," and therefore, "there is no universal preservation metadata element set" (2006). That being said, there are metadata standards that are commonly used for digital preservation. Two of the most widely adopted are outlined below.

PREMIS DATA DICTIONARY FOR PRESERVATION METADATA
The international working group PREMIS (PREservation Metadata: Implementation Strategies) created the PREMIS Data Dictionary for Preservation Metadata as a core set of metadata elements for the digital preservation community. "Core" in this instance is defined as "things that most working preservation repositories are likely to need to know in order to support digital preservation" (PREMIS Editorial Committee 2015). PREMIS is based on the conceptual model provided by the OAIS Reference Model, and one of the primary uses of PREMIS is for the exchange of archival information packages

between repositories. The PREMIS Data Dictionary defines "semantic units" rather than traditional metadata elements, and is implementation-neutral in that it focuses on defining *what* information should be recorded rather than on *how* it should be represented. Furthermore, these semantic units are mapped to "entities," or "things" that are described by preservation metadata. The five types of entities defined by the most current version of the data dictionary, PREMIS 3.0, are:

- *Object*—a discrete unit of information in digital form, that is, a file or bitstream;
- *Environment*—technology that supports an object in some way, that is, hardware or software for rendering or execution;
- *Event*—an action that affects objects in the repository, that is, migration or normalization;
- *Agent*—a person, organization, or software application that is involved in events or rights statements, that is, author or rights holder;
- *Rights Statement*—information about rights and permissions pertaining to objects in the repository.

A schema for representing PREMIS in XML exists at the Library of Congress PREMIS website (www.loc.gov/standards/premis), along with the PREMIS Data Dictionary. A helpful and accessible overview by Caplan can also be found on the website (Caplan 2009), although it does not reflect changes made to the data dictionary in its most recent update, version 3.0.

METADATA ENCODING AND TRANSMISSION SCHEMA

Another metadata standard that is highly used in digital preservation environments is the Metadata Encoding and Transmission Schema, or METS. METS is an XML-based framework for encoding various types of metadata associated with a digital object. It acts as a container or wrapper that allows for all types of metadata—descriptive, administrative, and structural—to be represented together in one XML document. The METS document is intended to package together information about the structure of the object, the names and locations of the files that comprise the object, and the metadata associated with the object; it is a good illustration of the concept of encapsulation described earlier in this chapter. The METS document contains sections for each of the following: descriptive metadata about the digital object, administrative metadata about the object, a list of files that make up the object, a structural map of the object's components, a list of links establishing relationships between the structural map's components, and lists of "behaviors" that may be associated with the object (i.e., pointers to programs or applications that are used to display the object). Metadata from various different schemas can be embedded or "nested" within each section, or the metadata may reside outside the document and be referenced via pointers.

For digital preservation purposes, the administrative metadata section of the METS document is most critical because it may contain information about file creation, format, provenance, copyright and licensing, and past transformations or migrations. PREMIS metadata may be integrated into the METS administrative metadata section, thus enabling for metadata exchange with other repositories. The Library of Congress PREMIS website offers guidelines for integrating PREMIS with METS at www.loc.gov/standards/premis/premis-mets.html. Like PREMIS, METS is compatible with the OAIS Reference Model, and in fact was designed to fulfill the OAIS "information package" concept. The METS schema and documentation, along with example METS documents and suggested readings, can be found at the Library of Congress's official METS website, www.loc.gov/standards/mets.

Digital Preservation at Smaller Institutions

While digital preservation is a relatively new field of practice, much progress has been made by the cultural heritage sector in developing guidelines and best practices for data curators to follow. But the successful application of digital preservation often relies on a certain level of resources that the small or midsized institution may lack: adequate staff; up-to-date technical infrastructure; expertise and knowledge of rapidly changing trends in the field; and, of course, sufficient funding. For professionals at smaller organizations, these factors can prove elusive or overwhelming when the time comes to plan and implement a local digital preservation program. So how does one make meaningful progress when resources are limited?

To begin with, it is important to keep in mind that digital preservation is not an all-or-nothing proposition, but rather an iterative process consisting of incremental and ongoing actions:

Practitioners don't have to start by creating or selecting a comprehensive solution and making hard and fast technology choices to be used for the next twenty years. They can start by taking small steps to prioritize and triage digital collections, while working to build awareness and advocate for resources. (Schumacher et al. 2014)

In other words, it is preferable to focus one's efforts on those activities that are within reach in the short term, rather than to wait for the "perfect" permanent solution to become available. Putting off doing *something*, however small, can result in irretrievable data loss in the long term.

Starting small and taking time to build up capacity is a wise approach for the smaller, resource-strapped institution. For the novice data steward, this raises the question of where to start and what constitutes the minimum steps to be taken. The National Digital Stewardship Alliance provides a useful framework that identifies four levels of digital preservation based on the functional areas of storage, fixity, security, metadata, and file formats. Beginning steps outlined in level one include taking an inventory of your digital assets, creating backup copies, creating fixity information, and moving files off of heterogeneous media formats and into a storage system. The guidelines are presented in the form of a rubric that can be used to plan and assess a digital preservation program that proceeds in stages (http://ndsa.org/activities/levels-of-digital-preservation). This tool can be a useful starting point for placing one's organization within the spectrum of digital preservation activities, and it provides a good baseline for starting a cumulative preservation program in which one level builds upon another over time.

In addition to embracing an incremental approach, it can also make sense to be selective regarding the level of preservation that is applied to different types of digital materials. Not all materials will necessarily require the same level of attention, and many institutions define various levels of preservation support that they will commit to providing for an object depending on its file type or format. For example, files that are in open, standard formats may receive a higher level of preservation support than those that are proprietary, and born-digital materials may be dealt with more rigorously than digitized materials for which there is an analog equivalent available. A higher level of support may include the maintenance of format integrity through such steps as migration and normalization, whereas a basic level of support may only entail ensuring access to the object in its original format. Prioritization of materials in this manner can help to streamline the preservation process and eliminate unnecessary effort for the small or under-resourced institution.

To further streamline the digital preservation process, there are tools available, in the form of software programs and commercial services, which automate preservation activities and workflows. Archivematica (www.archivematica.org) is a free and open source digital preservation system that assists users in performing a variety of actions on their digital resources, including creating copies, checking fixity, and normalizing and migrating files (there is also a hosted version of Archivematica available called ArchivesDirect, http://archivesdirect.org). The subscription service Duracloud (www.duracloud.org) offers many of the same file-processing abilities, along with storage for digital objects in the cloud. Preservica (http://preservica.com) is a hosted vendor solution that provides file processing and storage along with a public interface for accessing and displaying digital objects. Each of these tools, like the DCMS outlined in chapter 7, have their strengths and weaknesses in terms of ease of setup, technical expertise and infrastructure required, and cost.

If a full-scale digital preservation system is out of reach for your institution, other tools can be used as ad hoc solutions. For example, online cloud storage services, such as Amazon Glacier (https://aws.amazon.com/glacier), can provide cost-effective backup solutions for pennies per gigabyte per month. Another option that offers both off-site data storage and object display capabilities is the Internet Archive (https://archive.org/index.php), the nonprofit digital library introduced in chapter 4 which allows users to create free accounts and contribute their own digital content. Schumacher et al. suggest that this service "can serve as a very basic digital preservation tool for very small organizations" (2014), with the caveat that material uploaded to the site must be free of access restrictions (the organization must hold the rights to the content, or it must be in the public domain). The authors recommend using this or another online storage service in combination with Data Accessioner, a free tool that can be used to migrate content between media, create and validate checksums, and gather and compile metadata. According to the software's website (http://dataaccessioner.org), it is intended for use by smaller institutions that lack significant IT staff support. Many other tools exist that can be used to support various digital preservation functions, and a good place to find information about them is the Community Owned digital Preservation Tool Registry, or COPTR (http://coptr.digipres.org/Main_Page).

Finally, for the resource-challenged institution, collaboration can be the key to establishing and maintaining a sustainable digital preservation program. In fact, it can be asserted that a true digital preservation program requires multi-institutional collaboration, and that the most effective preservation efforts succeed through some strategy for distributing copies of content in secure, distributed geographic locations (Halbert and Skinner 2010). This concept of *distributed digital preservation* is exemplified by such initiatives as the MetaArchive Cooperative (www.metaarchive.org/), a network of libraries, archives, and other memory institutions from around the world in which member institutions store copies of each other's content on in-house servers. Distributed digital preservation networks such as this provide the advantage of allowing cultural heritage institutions to maintain ownership over their own digital content, rather than outsourcing it to commercial vendors. However, the technical infrastructure required to participate in such a network can be prohibitive for many smaller institutions. For these organizations, the best approach may be to take advantage of the cost savings that can be achieved by pooling funding and resources at the local or regional levels, for example by participating in a consortium-wide subscription to a third-party service such as DuraCloud.

Final Thoughts

Digital preservation is complex, both conceptually and in practice. A single chapter cannot do justice to the topic, and further study is advised for readers who wish to develop the knowledge required to implement a full-fledged digital preservation program at their institution. It can be all too easy to become overwhelmed to the point of inaction by the seeming enormity of the task, and for this reason many smaller institutions are at risk of falling behind in the race to keep our shared digital heritage available for future generations. But even those with the most basic knowledge of digital preservation can begin to take steps, however small, to safeguard their digital assets. The key may be to balance a sense of urgency with an acceptance that doing something is better than doing nothing. It can help to think of preservation as just another stage in the digitization process, one that is not optional, but necessary, and then to proceed to meet the challenge to the best of one's abilities.

REFERENCES

ALCTS Preservation and Reformatting Section. 2007. "Definitions of Digital Preservation." Chicago: Association for Library Collections & Technical Services. June 24. www.ala.org/alcts/resources/preserv/defdigpres0408.

Caplan, Priscilla. 2009. "Understanding PREMIS." Library of Congress PREMIS Official Website. https://www.loc.gov/standards/premis/understanding-premis.pdf.

———. 2006. "Preservation Metadata." In *DCC Curation Reference Manual,* edited by S. Ross and M. Day. www.dcc.ac.uk/resources/curation-reference-manual/completed-chapters/preservation-metadata.

Emory University's Stuart A. Rose Manuscript, Archives, and Rare Book Library. "The Digital Archives of Salman Rushdie." http://marbl.library.emory.edu/documents/digital-archives/rushdie-help-sheet.pdf.

Halbert, Martin, and Katherine Skinner. 2010. "Preserving Our Collections, Preserving Our Missions." In *A Guide to Distributed Digital Preservation,* edited by Katherine Skinner and Matt Schultz, 1–9. Atlanta: Educopia Institute. www.metaarchive.org/sites/metaarchive.org/files/GDDP_Educopia.pdf.

Harvey, Ross. 2010. *Digital Curation: A How-to-Do-It Manual.* New York: Neal-Schuman.

Kuny, Terry. 1997. "A Digital Dark Ages? Challenges in the Preservation of Information." 63rd IFLA Council and General Conference. http://archive.ifla.org/IV/ifla63/63kuny1.pdf.

Lavoie, Brian. 2014. *The Open Archival Information System Reference Model: Introductory Guide.* 2nd edition. DPC Technology Watch Series Report 14-02, Digital Preservation Coalition. doi: 10.7207/twr14-02.

Lavoie, Brian, and Richard Gartner. 2013. *Preservation Metadata.* 2nd edition. DPC Technology Watch Series Report 13-03, Digital Preservation Coalition. doi: 10.7207/twr13-03.

Library of Congress (LC) and National Institute of Standards and Technology (NIST). 2007. "Final Report: NIST/Library of Congress (LC) Optical Disc Longevity Study." https://www.loc.gov/preservation/resources/rt/NIST_LC_OpticalDiscLongevity.pdf.

Lunt, Barry M. 2011. "How Long Is Long-Term Data Storage?" Society for Imaging Science and Technology Archiving Conference. Salt Lake City, UT, May 16–19, 2011. www.imaging.org/site/PDFS/Reporter/Articles/2011_26/REP26_3_4_ARCH2011_Lunt.pdf.

National Digital Stewardship Alliance (NDSA). 2014. "Checking Your Digital Content." http://ndsa.org/documents/NDSA-Fixity-Guidance-Report-final100214.pdf.

PREMIS Editorial Committee. 2015. "PREMIS Data Dictionary for Preservation Metadata, Version 3.0." www.loc.gov/standards/premis/v3/premis-3-0-final.pdf.

Schumacher, Jaime, et al. 2014. "From Theory to Action: 'Good Enough' Digital Preservation Solutions for Under-Resourced Cultural Heritage Institutions." A Digital POWRR White Paper for the Institute of Museum and Library Services. http://commons.lib.niu.edu/bitstream/handle/10843/13610/FromTheoryToAction_POWRR_WhitePaper.pdf.?sequence=1.

Tonkin, Emma. 2008. "Persistent Identifiers: Considering the Options." *Ariadne* 56. www.ariadne.ac.uk/issue56/tonkin/#sthash.00sFaLK5.dpuf.

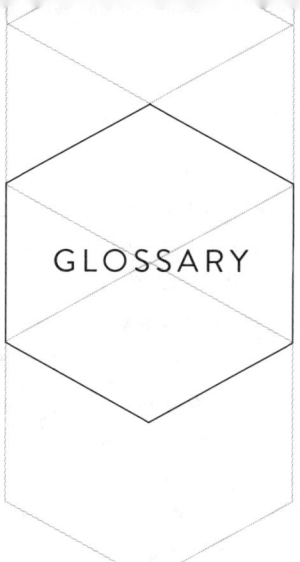

GLOSSARY

application profile. A set of domain-specific rules documenting a metadata scheme for a particular purpose, spelling out the element set and associated content guidelines (also known as a *data dictionary* or *best practice guide*).

attribute. In certain metadata schemes, such as MODS, VRA Core, and EAD, refinements to the meaning or scope of an element that contribute to greater granularity.

bit. Short for "binary digit," one of two digits (zero or one) in the binary system of notation; when combined into bitstreams they form the basis for a digital object.

bit depth. The number of bits allocated to an individual pixel in a digital image (also known as *color depth*).

bit rot. Physical decay to digital media at the bit level.

bitonal image. A digital image that has a bit depth of one, meaning it only has one bit available per pixel, which can contain one of two possible values (black or white).

bitstream copying. A digital preservation strategy that involves backing up a digital object by creating an exact bit-by-bit duplicate (also known as *replication* or *data redundancy*).

checksum. A unique sequence of letters and numbers, generated by a computer algorithm, which represents the bitstream of an individual digital file and can be used to verify fixity.

color channel. Where the color information for each of the primary color components is stored within a color model.

color model. A way to define color, describing how color will appear on paper (CMYK color model) or a computer screen (RGB color model).

color space. A defined range of colors that is available to a particular digital device or file (also known as *color profile*).

compression. A process for reducing the size of an image file, using an algorithm that reduces the amount of data required to represent the image.

crosswalk. A table or other visual representation that shows how elements from two or more different metadata schemes are mapped to each other.

derivative image. A digital image created from a master file and used for specific purposes including access copies for online viewing and thumbnails for image browsing within a DCMS.

digital content management system (DCMS). A software used to store, manage, and deliver digital content.

Dublin Core Metadata Element Set (DCMES). An all-purpose metadata standard consisting of fifteen core metadata elements that can be extended through the use of qualifiers or refinements.

emulation. A digital preservation strategy in which the look and feel of a digital object is re-created through the use of software that mimics obsolete applications, operating systems, or hardware architecture.

encapsulation. A digital preservation strategy that entails the grouping together of a digital object in its original form as a bitstream, along with information necessary to decode and render the object in the future.

Encoded Archival Description (EAD). A metadata standard used to encode archival finding aids in XML to make them searchable and browseable online.

Extensible Markup Language (XML). A markup language that can be used to encode metadata for machine processing and exchange.

fair use. A doctrine codified in Section 107 of U.S. copyright law that allows for the reproduction, distribution, or performance of a copyrighted work for certain purposes, based on a weighing of four factors related to the nature of the copyrighted work and the intended use.

fixity checking. A digital preservation strategy used to verify the bit-level integrity and stability of a digital file over time, commonly performed through the use of checksums.

granularity. The level of detail with which a resource or collection is described.

Graphics Interchange Format (GIF). An image file format that uses lossless compression, allows for eight-bit grayscale or color, and can be used to create simple animations.

grayscale image. A digital image that can contain the range of neutral shades between black and white, typically containing a bit depth of two to sixteen bits.

institutional repository. A digital archive of the intellectual product created by the faculty, research staff, and students of an institution, typically associated with academic institutions.

interoperability. The ability of multiple systems to exchange data with minimal loss of information and functionality.

Joint Photographic Experts Group (JPEG). A lossy compression technique and image file format commonly applied to grayscale and color images and often used to create derivative images for web access.

lossless compression. A file compression technique in which all data is retained and image quality is maintained, resulting in a large file size.

lossy compression. A file compression technique in which a smaller file size is achieved by discarding the least significant data in the image, resulting in a loss of image quality.

master image. A high-quality digital version of an analog object that is stored for purposes of long-term archiving and preservation and used to produce derivative images for web delivery.

metadata. Structured data that is associated with an information resource.

metadata element. A descriptive property of an information resource, represented by a predefined field that may be given a range of values.

Metadata Encoding and Transmission Schema (METS). An XML-based metadata standard that allows for descriptive, administrative, and structural metadata about a digital object to be packaged together.

Metadata Object Description Schema (MODS). A highly granular metadata standard that is derived from the MARC 21 Format for Bibliographic Data.

metadata scheme. A structured set of metadata elements designed for a specific purpose, such as describing a particular type of information source; an implementation of a metadata standard (also known as an *element set*).

metadata standard. A set of guidelines or specifications for metadata structure or content; may be a scheme that has been developed and maintained by a standard organization or other group.

migration. A digital preservation strategy in which a digital object is converted from a hardware or software that is at risk of becoming obsolete, to a more current technology; also a general term used to describe moving digital content from one software platform to another.

normalization. A digital preservation strategy in which digital objects are converted to a more preservation-friendly file format (typically from a proprietary format to an open one).

Open Archival Information System (OAIS) Reference Model. An international standard that provides a conceptual framework for the design and implementation of digital archival systems dedicated to preserving and maintaining access to digital information over the long term.

Open Archives Initiative Protocol for Metadata Harvesting (OAI-PMH). A mechanism for repository interoperability that allows for metadata sharing between systems, in which "data providers" expose their metadata to harvesting by "service providers."

open source. Software that is openly available on the Internet and can generally be downloaded and used without a fee, allowing users to modify the source code.

optical character recognition (OCR). Software that converts images of words and letters into machine-readable text files that can be indexed for searching.

orphan work. A work which may be protected by copyright, but for which the rights holder cannot be identified or located.

persistent identifier (PID). A unique sequence of alphanumeric characters that is assigned to a digital object and is permanently associated with the object throughout its life span, independent of name or address changes.

pixel. A physical point in a raster image, arranged in a grid of rows and columns, that is the basic unit of programmable color.

Portable Document Format (PDF). An open file format that allows for full-text search capability and is a de facto standard for delivering documents on the Web.

Portable Network Graphics (PNG). An open file format that is widely used for delivering images on the Web.

PREMIS Data Dictionary for Preservation Metadata. An international metadata standard for supporting the preservation of digital objects, based on the OAIS Reference Model.

raster image. A digital image comprised of pixels, resulting from the conversion of analog data into digital data by a measuring process known as sampling.

refinement. A subproperty used in the Dublin Core metadata standard to extend and refine the fifteen core elements and give them a greater degree of granularity (also known as a qualifier).

refreshing. A digital preservation strategy involving the bit-level copying of a digital object by transferring data between two types of the same long-term storage medium.

spatial resolution. The level of spatial detail a digital raster image contains, expressed in pixels per inch (ppi).

Tagged Image File Format (TIFF). An open image file format that supports both lossy and lossless compression and is typically used for capturing high-quality master images.

Visual Resource Association (VRA) Core. A metadata standard generally used to describe works of visual culture such as art and architecture.

INDEX

f denotes figures; *t* denotes tables. Boldface indicates a glossary definition.

# #
8-bit grayscale, 70, 77*t*
24-bit color, 70, 77*t*

A
academic libraries
    case studies of, 41–44, 60
    challenges facing, 7–8, 16
    institutional repositories and, 115, 118–119, **173**
    surveys of, 3, 29, 35–36, 126
    See also libraries; smaller institutions
accessibility, digitization to improve, 5
added-value features, 3, 6
administrative metadata, 90, 161, 164
administrators, collaboration with, 39
Adobe Acrobat, 73, 82
Adobe Photoshop, 78
advocacy, 29–30
Amazon Glacier, 166
Anglo-American Cataloging Rules (AACR), 92
application profiles, 91, 104, 106*t*–107*t*, **171**
Archivematica, 166
archives
    collaboration with staff in, 36–37, 41
    software for, 116–117, 123–124
    See also smaller institutions
ArchivesDirect, 166
Artists Rights Society, 144
Asana, 27
Association for Library Collections and Technical Services (ALCTS), 155
Association of College and Research Libraries (ACRL), 3
attributes, 96–98, **171**
Authors Guild v. Google, 53, 147
Authors Registry, 144
autodidacticism, 23–24

B
Barrow, William, 41
Berne Convention, 138–139
best practices
    for collaborative project management, 44–48
    documentation of, 103–104
    for image conversion, 67–68, 73–79, 84–85
bit depth, 69–70, 76, 77*t*, **171**
bit rot, 153–154, 159, **171**
bitonal images, 69, 76, 77*t*, **171**
bits (binary digits), 68–70, **171**

178 \ INDEX

bitstream copying, 157-158, **171**
BloggERS!, 32
blogs, recommended, 32-33
Boock, Michael, 41
Borges, Jorge Luis, 51
Breeding, Marshall, 9-10
budgets and funding, 8-10, 12-13, 61

C

Calhoun, Karen, 16
cameras, 80
Caplan, Priscilla, 162-163
Cataloging Cultural Objects (CCO), 92
Cervone, H. Frank, 44, 126
Chapman, Stephen, 5, 7
check-ins and meetings, 46-47
checksums, 159, **172**
Cleveland State University Library, 41-42
cloud computing, 13-14, 120, 166
CMYK color model, 70, **172**
Code Academy, 24
Code4Lib Journal, 32
Cohen, Daniel J., 82
collaboration
    cross-departmental, 27-28, 35-48
    cross-institutional, 28-29, 52-63, 167
    as essential skill, 27-28
    potential collaborators for, 36-40
    in project management, 44-48
    pros and cons of, 61-63
collection development departments, 38-39, 41-42
collective licensing agencies, 143-144
CollectiveAccess, 123-124
"College Librarians and the University-Library Syndrome" (Farber), 7
college libraries. *See* academic libraries
color channels, 70, **172**
color images, 69-70, 72-73, 75-76, 77*t*, **172**
color models, 70, **172**
color spaces, 70, **172**
commercial software, 113-117, 125-127, 129
communication, as essential skill, 29-30, 45-47
community engagement, 16
Community Owned digital Preservation Tool Registry (COPTR), 167
compression, 70-73, **172-173**
computer monitors, 70, 81-82
Computers in Libraries, 32

conservators, collaboration with, 39
consortia, collaboration in, 10, 57-60, 121
content aggregation, 58-59
content hubs, 56
content management systems. *See* digital collection management systems (DCMSs)
CONTENTdm, 14, 114-115
controlled vocabularies, 92, 102-103, 106*t*-107*t*, 114
conversion. *See* image conversion
copyright
    basics of, 133-139
    exemptions from, 136, 139-141
    infringement of, 53, 135, 139-141, 142, 147-148
    orphan works and, 141-142, 145, 148-149, **174**
    permissions and, 141, 142-146
    risk management and, 135, 146-149
Copyright Act, 135-137, 139-141
Copyright Clearance Center, 144
Copyright Office, 136, 137, 142, 143
Corbett, Hillary, 127
Cornell University, 120, 156
corruption of media, 153-155, 159
Coyle, Karen, 52
Creative Commons, 137-138
Crews, Kenneth D., 149
cross-departmental collaboration, 27-28, 35-48
cross-institutional collaboration, 28-29, 52-63, 167
crosswalks, 105, 108t, **172**
crowdsourcing, 15
cultural heritage institutions
    copyright and, 134, 139-141, 146-149
    cross-departmental collaboration in, 27-28, 35-48
    cross-institutional collaboration among, 28-29, 52-63
    patron expectations of, vii, 4, 6, 7-8
    potential collaborators in, 36-40
    preservation and, 152-153, 164-167
    See also smaller institutions
curators, collaboration with, 36-37

D

Data Accessioner, 166
data content standards, 92, 102-103

data format standards, 92
data loss, 153–155, 158–159
data structure standards, 92–100
data value standards, 92, 102
databases. *See* digital collection management systems (DCMSs)
DCMSs. *See* digital collection management systems (DCMSs)
decision-making process, 46–47
delegation, as essential skill, 21–22
departments, collaboration between, 27–28, 35–48
derivative image files, 74–75, 77–78, **172**
descriptive metadata, 89–90, 161
deterioration of media, 151, 153–155
digital collection management systems (DCMSs)
 collaboration on, 37–38, 41–42, 59–60
 defined, 112, **172**
 open source, 8, 14, 113, 118–124, 125–127, 129
 options for, 113–124
 proprietary, 113–117, 125–127, 129
 selection and evaluation of, 111–112, 124–130
 vendors and, 14–15, 113, 126, 128*t*
Digital Commons, 115–116
digital dark age, 152
digital librarians
 perceptions of, 19
 potential collaborators for, 36–40
 skills essential for, 21–30
 at smaller institutions, 11
 as solo practitioners, 20–32
 See also librarians
digital libraries
 challenges facing, 16
 collaborative, 55–61
 patron expectations of, vii, 4, 6, 7–8
 See also academic libraries; libraries
digital photos. *See* images, digital
digital preservation
 collaboration in, 59, 167
 defined, 155–157
 vs. digitization for preservation, 5–6, 155
 media degradation and, 151, 153–155, 157
 metadata for, 160–164
 recommended resources for, 33
 at smaller institutions, 164–168
 strategies for, 157–160
 technological obsolescence and, 152, 154–155, 157–158, 160
Digital Preservation Management Workshop, 156
Digital Preservation Matters, 33
Digital Public Library of America (DPLA), 55–56
digital repository systems, 112
digitization
 defined, 4
 isolation of, 19–20
 large-scale collaborative projects, 54–57
 mass digitization projects, 52–54
 outsourcing of, 80, 83–84
 reasons for, 4–7
 recommended resources for, 32–33
 at smaller institutions, 4–17
Digitization 101 blog, 33
distributed digital preservation, 167
D-Lib Magazine, 33
documentation, creation of, 26, 46, 103–104
Doherty, Brian, 16
Drupal, 112, 121, 123
DSpace, 118–120
Dublin Core Metadata Element Set (DCMES), 93, 94–95*t*, 101, 105, 108*t*, 119, 123, **172**
Duracloud, 166
DuraSpace, 120

E

Eastern Illinois University, 43
electronic resource librarians, 38
elements, metadata, 91–105, 108*t*, **173**
Emory University, 158
emulation, 158, **172**
encapsulation, 158–159, 163, **172**
Encoded Archival Description (EAD), 99–100, **172**
error messages, 31
Europeana, 55–56
evaluation
 of software, 127–130
 of workflows, 47–48
experimentation, as essential skill, 25
Extensible Markup Language (XML), 22, 91, 92, 95, 100, 163, 172

F

fair use doctrine, 140, 148, **172**
Farber, Evan Ira, 7, 15-16
Fedora, 120-122
file formats, for images, 71-73
file naming conventions, 78-79
film scanners, 80-81
first sale doctrine, 134-135
fixity checking, 159, **173**
flatbed scanners, 79-80, 81
flexibility, as essential skill, 25
funding, 8-10, 12-13, 61

G

Galvin, Denis, 14
Gartner, Richard, 160
Gathegi, John N., 149
German, Elizabeth M., 45
GIF files, 72-73, 74-75, **173**
Gilliland, Anne J., 92
GIMP, 78
Google Books, 53-54, 57, 147
grant funding, 9, 12-13, 61
granularity, 91, 93, **173**
graphic designers, collaboration with, 37
Graphics Interchange Format (GIF), 72-73, 74-75, **173**
Graveline, Jeffrey D., 146
grayscale images, 69-70, 72, 76, 77*t*, **173**
Greenstone, 118
Griffy, Henry, 127
Gueguen, Gretchen, 35

H

Hamilton, Val, 16
Hanlon, Ann M., 35
hardware, for image conversion, 12, 79-82
HathiTrust, 56-57
Hirtle, Peter, 137, 147
Hudson, Emily, 147
Huwe, Terence K., 6
Hydra, 122

I

image conversion
    best practices, 67-68, 73-79, 84-85
    hardware for, 12, 79-82
    outsourcing of, 83-84
images, digital
    compression, 70-73, **172-173**
    defined, 68-71
    file formats, 71-73
    master and derivative files, 74-75, 77*t*
    preservation of, 152, 161
    resolution and color, 69-70, 75-77
independent learning, 23-24
information technology (IT) professionals, 13, 38
infrastructure, 8, 12-15
Institute of Museum and Library Services, 9, 122
institutional repositories (IRs), 115, 118-119, **173**
institutions. *See* cultural heritage institutions; smaller institutions
intellectual property. *See* copyright
interdepartmental collaboration, 27-28, 35-48
interest in technology, as essential skill, 22-23
International Organization for Standardization (ISO), 73, 93, 106*t*
Internet Archive, 54, 56, 57, 143, 166
interoperability, 104-105, **173**
interpersonal skills, 29-30
interpolation, 78
IrfanView, 78
irrelevancy reduction, 71
Islandora, 14, 121

J

Jeppesen, Bruce, 41
Joint Photographic Experts Group (JPEG), 72, 74-75, **173**
journals, recommended, 32-33
JPEG 2000 files, 72, 75
JPEG files, 72, 74-75, 173

K

Kahle, Brewster, 54
Kenyon, Andrew T., 147
Kucsma, Jason, 123
Kunda, Sue, 45-46
Kuny, Terry, 152

L

Lagoze, Carl, 120
Lampert, Corey, 45

INDEX / 181

Lankes, R. David, 16
Lavoie, Brian, 159, 160
LeFurgy, Bill, 22–23
Levy, David M., 7
librarians
   attitudes of, 7
   mission of, 16
   at smaller institutions, 11
   as solo practitioners, 20–32
   See also digital librarians
libraries
   case studies of, 41–44, 60
   collaborative digital libraries, 55–61
   community engagement and, 16
   patron expectations of, vii, 4, 6, 7–8
   surveys of, 3, 29, 35–36, 126
   See also academic libraries; smaller institutions
Library of Alexandria, 51
"The Library of Babel" (Borges), 51
Library of Congress
   blog posts by, 22–23, 33
   digital initiatives of, 56
   on media degradation, 154
   metadata standards of, 95, 97, 99, 102, 163–164
Library of Congress Subject Headings (LCSH), 92, 102
Library Services and Technology Act, 12–13
licensed proprietary software, 113–117, 125–127, 129
licenses, Creative Commons, 137–138*f*
local history collections, 15–16
local partnerships, 60–61
lossless compression, 71–73, **173**
lossy compression, 71–72, **173**
LUNA, 117
Lynda, 24

M

Machine-Readable Cataloging (MARC) records, 88–89, 92, 95
mapping, 105, 108*t*
mass digitization projects, 52–54
master image files, 74–75, 77*t*, **173**
McGlone, Jonathan, 20
media degradation, 151, 153–155, 157
meetings and check-ins, 46–47
mentoring, 29

MetaArchive Cooperative, 167
metadata
   defined, 88–89, **173**
   for digital preservation, 160–164
   importance of, 87–88
   schemes for, 91, 92, 100–109, **173**
   standards for, 91–100, 162–164, **174**
   terminology for, 90–91
   types of, 89–90
Metadata Encoding and Transmission Schema (METS), 163–164, **173**
Metadata Object Description Schema (MODS), 95–97*t*, 108*t*, **173**
Michener, James, 104, 106*t*–107*t*
microfilm and microfiche, 77*t*, 81
Middle Tennessee State University, 60
Middleton, Ken, 60
migration, 157–158, 160, **174**
Miller, Paul, 88
money and funding, 8–10, 12–13, 61
monitors, 70, 81–82
Mountain West Digital Library (MWDL), 59, 108
museums
   metadata for, 97–99*t*, 102
   software for, 116–117, 123–124
   See also smaller institutions
musical works, 144

N

National Digital Stewardship Alliance, 165
National Information Standards Organization (NISO), 93
National Institute of Standards and Technology (NIST), 13–14, 154
negatives and slides, 77*t*, 80–81
networking, as essential skill, 28–29
normalization, 160, 174

O

Omeka, 14, 122–123
Online Computer Library Center (OCLC), 4, 93, 114
online courses, 24
Open Archival Information System (OAIS) Reference Model, 159, 164, **174**
Open Archives Initiative Protocol for Metadata Harvesting (OAI-PMH), 55, **174**

Open Content Alliance (OCA), 53-54
open source software, 8, 14, 31, 113,
    118-124, 125-127, 129, **174**
optical character recognition (OCR), 3, 82,
    174
Oregon State University Libraries, 43-44
orphan works, 141-142, 145, 148-149,
    174
outsourcing, 80, 83-84
overhead scanners, 80
oversized materials, 77t, 80
ownership, identifying, 142-145

P
Paint.NET, 78
participatory librarianship, 16
partnerships. See collaboration
PastPerfect, 116, 123-124
patrons, expectations of, vii, 4, 6, 7-8
PDF files, 73, **174**
periodicals, recommended, 32-33
permissions, obtaining, 141, 142-146
persistent identifiers (PIDs), 162, **174**
Photoshop, 78
pictures. See images
Piper, Alison, 16
pixels, 68-70, 77-78, **174**
policies and procedures, 46-48
Portable Document Format (PDF), 73, **174**
Portable Network Graphics (PNG), 72-73,
    75, **174**
ppi (pixels per inch), 69, 75-76, 77t
PREMIS, 163-164, **175**
preplanning stage, 44-45
preservation
    digitization as tool for, 5-6, 155
    See also digital preservation
preservationists, collaboration with, 39
Preservica, 166
Prilop, Valerie, 45
prioritization, 26, 46-47
processing images, 77-78
professional organizations, 24, 29
professionals, in digitization. See digital
    librarians
project management
    collaborative, 44-48
    as essential skill, 20, 25-27
    strategies for, 26-27
proprietary software, 113-117, 125-127, 129

public domain, 137-139, 148-149
public libraries. See libraries

Q
qualifiers, 93-95t

R
Raab, Christopher, 61
raster images, 68, **175**
recommended resources, 32-33
records, defined, 91
redundancy reduction, 71
refinements, 93-95t, **175**
refreshing, 157, **175**
regional collaborative projects, 57-60
Reiss, Kevin, 123
repositories, collaborative, 55-60
reproduction rights organizations, 143-144
resizing images, 77-78
resolution, 69, 75-78, 79-80, **175**
RGB color model, 70, 77t, **172**
rights management metadata, 161
rights of ownership, identifying, 142-145
Riley, Jenn, 92
risk management, 135, 146-149
Rosenzweig, Roy, 82
Russell, Carrie, 149

S
Salman Rushdie Digital Archives Project,
    158
sampling, 68-69
Samuels, Ruth Gallegos, 127
scaling, 4
scanners, for image conversion, 12, 79-81
schemes, metadata, 91, 92, 100-109, **173**
Schumacher, Jaime, 166
"Seeing Standards" (Riley), 92
self-advocacy, 29-30
self-directed learning, 23-24
servers and networks, 13-15, 125-126
service hubs, 56
Sidman, Angela, 123
The Signal blog, 22-23, 33
skills, essential, 21-30
slides and negatives, 77t, 80-81
smaller institutions
    advantages of, 15-16
    challenges facing, vii-viii, 4, 7-12, 17
    infrastructure of, 8, 12-15

preservation and, 152–153, 164–167
staffing of, 10–12
See also cultural heritage institutions; libraries
Society of American Archivists, 32, 99, 145
software
    cost considerations and, 8, 14, 125–126
    for editing images, 78
    obsolescence of, 152, 154–155, 158
    open source, 8, 14, 113, 118–124, 125–127, 129, **174**
    for preservation, 166–167
    for project management, 27
    proprietary, 113–117, 125–127, 129
    troubleshooting of, 31
    See also specific software
solo digital librarians. *See* digital librarians
sovereign immunity, 140–141
spatial resolution, 69, 76, **175**
special collections department, collaboration with, 36–37, 41–42
SQL (Structured Query Language), 24
staffing considerations, 10–12, 43
standards, metadata, 91–100, 162–164, **174**
state collaborative projects, 57–60
Stein, Ayla, 126
structural metadata, 90, 161
Structured Query Language (SQL), 24
Sun, Mang, 14
support staff, delegation to, 21–22
sustainability, 16
systems departments, collaboration with, 37–38, 42

T

Tagged Image File Format (TIFF), 71–72, 74–75, **175**
Taylor, Mayo, 60
technical infrastructure, 8, 12–15
technical metadata, 161
technical services, collaboration with, 37, 41, 43
technological obsolescence, 152, 154–155, 157–158, 160
technology, interest in, 22–23
Tesseract, 82
thesauri, 92, 102, 114
Thompson, Santi, 126
three-legged stool visual, 156*f*
TIFF files, 71–72, 74–75, **175**

tonality, 69–70
Tonkin, Emma, 162
tracking systems, 27
transparency, fostering, 46
Trello, 27
troubleshooting, art of, 30–32

U

United Nations Educational, Cultural, and Scientific Organization (UNESCO), 56, 118
university libraries. *See* academic libraries
University of Denver Penrose Library, 43
University of Houston Libraries, 42
University of Maryland Libraries, 42–43
university-library syndrome, 7
unpublished works, 136, 138, 139, 144
U.S. Copyright Office, 136, 137, 142, 143

V

value-added features, 3, 6
values, metadata, 91–92, 102–103
Vaughan, Jason, 45
Vavra, Robert, 104, 106*t*–107*t*
vendors, working with, 14–15, 83–84, 113, 126, 128*t*, 129
Visual Artists and Galleries Association, 144
Visual Resource Association (VRA) Core Categories, 97–99*t*, **175**
Volunteer Voices, 60
volunteers, delegation to, 21–22

W

W3schools, 24
WATCH File, 143
web services staff, collaboration with, 37
Webopedia, 33
websites
    for independent learning, 24
    of recommended resources, 32–33
Westbrook, R. Niccole, 45
willingness to experiment, as essential skill, 25
WordPress, 112, 123
workflows, interdepartmental, 40–45, 47–48
World Digital Library (WDL), 56

X

XML (Extensible Markup Language), 22, 91, 92, 95, 100, 163, **172**